Hawai'i Calling

THE HALI'A ALOHA SERIES

Hawai'i Calling

RIC D. STARK

LEGACY ISLE
PUBLISHING

THE HALI'A ALOHA SERIES
Darien Hsu Gee, Series Editor

Hali'a Aloha ("cherished memories") by Legacy Isle Publishing is a guided memoir program developed in collaboration with series editor Darien Hsu Gee. The series celebrates moments big and small, harnessing the power of short forms to preserve the lived experiences of the storytellers. To become a Hali'a Aloha author, please visit www.legacyislepublishing.net.

Legacy Isle Publishing is an imprint of Watermark Publishing, based in Honolulu, Hawai'i, and dedicated to "Telling Hawai'i's Stories" through memoirs, corporate biographies, family histories and other books.

ISBN 978-1-948011-58-7 (print)
ISBN 978-1-948011-59-4 (ebook)

Design and production
Dawn Sakamoto Paiva

Legacy Isle Publishing
1000 Bishop St., Ste. 806
Honolulu, HI 96813
Telephone 1-808-587-7766
Toll-free 1-866-900-BOOK
www.legacyislepublishing.net

Printed in the United States

He Hoʻomanaʻo

In memory of
George Luther Glasener,
my maternal grandfather,
koʻu kumu (my source);
the man I idolized in childhood,
a man whom I would become so unlike in adulthood;
the man I look to,
a man I love—forever.

CONTENTS

FOREWORD

In the title of this book, *Hawaiʻi Calling*, "calling" is a verb, specifically a gerund of the action word "call." Ric's implication is that the state, the geographic island chain, the culture, and people are crying out to him, shouting his name, welcoming his *mana*, enticing him with sights, smells, and sounds.

I've known Ric for decades. I first knew him via my mom, who often texted me clever wordplay jokes Ric made when they worked together serving the people of Oʻahu who needed help with their health. Now he texts my children directly, consulting them as his own personal Urban Dictionary and social justice warriors. He's undeniably smart and funny, but Ric is also someone I'm always happy to sit down and talk with, about anything. Three generations of my family agree that Ric has interesting opinions and is an asset to any dinner party!

Ric's book is a gorgeous collection of memories, chicken-skin experiences, and talk-story morsels, giving us glimpses into a man who stitched words from his heart into this beautiful quilt of his life. It is an homage to his provenance, joy about where he is, and speculation on where he may yet go. He shares amazing people and places. He shows us in detail how the experiences changed him. Let his stories waft over you like a cool trade wind breeze, and listen to Ric's truth: sometimes funny, occasionally sad, always genuine. Come, hear the calling.

Pennington Ahlstrand Neuhaus
Northern California, April 2021

INTRODUCTION

"Oh no! He thinks I want to talk to him about being a queer!" No idea how I knew, but I did. Mr. Ridge thought I had asked to see him to announce that I was homosexual.

My words had aimed nowhere near his mark. "I want to thank you for being such a great teacher. You encouraged my creative writing, and that was such a gift. You are the best teacher I've ever had, and I want you to know that."

"Oh! Well, thank you. Uhh, yes, you were a great student, and I was happy to encourage you." After a long pause, relief flooded across Roy Ridge's face. "You know, I really thought you were going to talk about something else."

There was something in his manner, a heightened tension I had sensed immediately upon entering his classroom. His feminine features fidgeted more than usual when he stood—too stilted—behind his desk. His manicured fingers grasped his chair as if he needed to brace himself for our encounter.

On my first break from freshman year at Macalester College, I had asked to talk with my favorite teacher. I was his student in high school for two years of German and senior English Literature, where we were assigned a weekly composition. I loved that class. With Roy Ridge's encouragement, I opened my creative mind, tackling each assignment with famished relish.

The awkwardness of our meeting became mutual. Determined that the topic of sexuality must remain unmentionable, I spoke in a clumsy attempt to smooth over our discomforts. "Well, I just needed to tell you how much I appreciated you, especially how you encouraged my writing."

Alarmed by our exchange of unspoken thoughts about sexuality, I hastened my exit. Disappointed—I had failed to convey the depth of my gratitude.

Mr. Ridge had opened many windows into my private sanctum. How far could I reach into the untapped energies of my mind? Mr. Ridge had encouraged me to discover my voice. The queer thing? He was nine years too early on that one.

. . .

"D minus? He must be kidding. I'm class valedictorian. I had a 4.0 GPA!" I slammed the paper face down on my desk. I didn't hear one word in class.

Campus rumor had it that freshman English Comp was the winnowing course, designed to get rid of the students who couldn't rise to the mark. Requiring strict adherence to in-the-box assignments,

Mr. Mueller had graded C's on my first two writing compositions.

Now a D minus? Frustrated and frantic, I turned to the next assignment without enthusiasm, penned in rote, adhering to Don Kee Mueller's assigned instructions. Finishing the task in fifteen minutes with zero effort (and none of Ric), I submitted my next paper. Mueller graded it with an A. Each week the same, I aced the course.

My flaming desire to write thwarted, I never took another English class at Mac.

. . .

Roy Ridge had engendered a new creative writer. Under Don Kee Mueller's instruction, a young mind had learned about valuing conformity over creativity. Fifty years later, the phoenix rises with all the fire and flamboyance of Conchita Wurst. (Google her. Really! Google "Conchita Wurst, Rise Like a Phoenix, Austria, 2014.")

And the queer thing? While this memoir is not about "my life as a gay man," the undercurrent pervades. My sister-in-law missed the mark quite widely when she declared, "We don't talk about what we do in the bedroom. Why do you need to?" Indeed, being gay isn't a recreational bedroom activity. It's a way of being.

Chapter One

WINTER RAINBOW

An Ad in This Morning's Paper. Round Trip, Fourteen Nights—550 Bucks

"Nooo way." Disbelieving but intrigued, I challenged Chuck. I hated winters, but this was too good.

"I'm reading it as we speak," Chuck cajoled over the phone. A friend who rented a room in my two-bedroom home in South Minneapolis, Chuck had risen early Sunday morning and purchased his newspaper and coffee. Sipping caffeine in his law office while scanning the paper, he had discovered a winter rainbow!

An hour later I heard the rustle at the back door, the stomping of feet to shake off the February snow, then the *clump, clump, clump* up the back steps. Bustling through the kitchen, Chuck persisted, "So what do you think?"

"I have two weeks of vacation approved by my boss. Sit. We need to book our flights." The embodiment of fiery Leo energy, I live by an adventurous motto: "Jump first, then ask, 'Where we going?'"

Was there any question? It was mid-February in Minnesota, a bright sun-lit morning but fifteen degrees outdoors. I hate winter and that ole man retained his firm grip on the northland. It was 1986 and I had lived in Minnesota for nineteen years. I had adapted to a world of six-month winters with long dark evenings by cuddling up in draft-chilled houses, stitching needlepoint, knitting, macrame, weaving. Several times a week I clamped on cross-country skis and enjoyed outdoor sports. I tried winter fishing—too boring. Attempted winter camping where I pitched a tent atop the snow beside some frozen lake and slept in a down-filled sleeping bag on the ground at five degrees above or below zero. No, thank you!

So a two-week winter vacation in Hawai'i in March for $550?!? Minutes after Chuck peeled off his winter coat, we were booked on a no-frills economy flight. Minneapolis to Honolulu, March 21, 1986. Aloha, here we come!

Plane Tickets Purchased

One interminable month before we would fly. Hawai'i—winter escape. Hawai'i—sun and sand in *March*. Hawai'i—blue, blue ocean. Hawai'i—home to Michener's mixed-blood golden people. Hawai'i—shirtless brown men. Hawai'i—outdoor gay bars and gay beaches. Hawai'i—winter playground.

Determined to stand out in the Waikīkī night scene, I dedicated inordinate hours in March to purchasing my wardrobe. I bought six or eight ensembles of casual shirts in soft periwinkle blues, jade greens, and peach-tone pinks with the perfect Bermuda shorts in three shades of beige. Capping off my wardrobe, I purchased a snappy, peach-colored sport coat with off-white cotton pants.

Minnesota shopping, California colors, snappy attire—all set to attract notice. All of it simply WROoooNnG!

On our first night, I wore that peach outfit to the gay bar in Waikīkī. Seconds after entering Hamburger Mary's, I scolded myself, "Ohhhh, Ric! You should have done some homework." Local guys wore T-shirts and gym shorts with slippahs on the night scene. Any man in a sport coat, long pants, and Oxford shoes was screaming, "Tourista!" (Or in Hawaiian, "*Malihini*!") On day two, stylish outfits back in the suitcase, I ducked into an ABC Store and bought elastic shorts and flip-flops.

The wardrobe misjudgment is a perfect metaphor for my life in Hawai'i these thirty-four years and how I've had to grapple with this dichotomy. I answered with enthusiasm the deep, undeniable call of my spirit to live in this tropical home. Yet once here, I am forever just one more *haole* boy from the Midwest mainland. Wrong clothes, wrong slippahs, wrong manners, wrong skin.

Thirty-four years later…I'm no more Hawaiian than Justin Blake.[1]

---

1. Transgender TikTok star, born in Minnesota, February 1, 2000.

Growing Up

Dad was present and truly engaged with his family on two occasions annually, New Year's Eve and summer vacation. Every June we enjoyed a week-long stay at Grandpa Glasener's cabin on the southern shore of Lake Superior. Bark Point has a USGS marker on its wide, flat rock. It's even identified on some US maps.

While excitement was building as vacation week approached, our family dreaded packing and departing. Mom and Dad argued. Silly details were contested. Leaving on time was fraught with tension and spats. Inevitably we all climbed into the car— Mom and Dad in front, three boys and the family dog crammed into the back seat.

The eight-hour drive from northeastern Iowa to Lake Superior was agonizingly interminable for us boys. We played countless car games—counting tractors or spotting A to Z of the alphabet on billboards. "Q" spotted only on a Quaker State Oil sign. Passing through Spooner, Wisconsin, the lush rolling farmlands of Iowa and Wisconsin gave way to flat, impoverished fields of the north. Farm fields yielded to forests of pine and birch.

Peering over Dad's shoulder, I ached to catch that first glimpse of the lake—a distinct, dark blue on the horizon. Every year I expected that first sight would appear at least an hour before we arrived. And every year, eyes strained and neck craned, I would finally call out, "There it is, Mom! Lake Superior!"

Turning east on Highway 13, Dad pulled off the highway at the first open spot along the shoreline.

Scrambling out of the car, my brothers and I bounded across the sandy beach to touch the chilly water, skip a flat stone out into the lake, and peer in wonder across the vast span of Lake Superior, our summer home.

"Ric, don't let the dog get wet. She'll get sand all over the car," Mom called, trying in vain. In a moment, moods altered. It was something about the lake—she enchanted us with her limitless expanse, her endless hypnotizing waves, her healing energy. She brought our family close, if only for one week.

The half-hour drive along the south shore brought a cacophony of joyful laughter. Impatience finally yielded to the dirt lane and driveway into Bark Point. Clambering out of the car, we sprinted down the path toward the quaint pine cabin. A few steps further, we halted at the twenty-foot-high cliff above the stony shore of Lake Superior.

That first breath would stun me. Inhaling deeply, I could smell that cool, crisp scent of north woods pine. Paused, I would fill my ears and my heart with the drumbeat of crashing waves. Then we all scrambled into Grandpa's cabin with its familiar yet strange woodsy smell, our family home for the next week.

Breakfasts were Dad's purview—eggs and bacon and toast or pancakes with orange juice—cooked to perfection by the chef. For a whole week, Dad would be present and share with our family in north woods adventures. Boating on the lake was unpredictable: sometimes calm, other times heaving with treacherous waves. Fishing on Lake Superior where only Grandpa and Uncle Dale caught whitefish. Fishing Iron River where we boys filled the stringers with bluegills and perch. Day trips to the harbor towns of Cornucopia and Bayfield. A ferry ride through the Apostle Islands.

It always delighted me. For just a few days, I could feel the contentment of being the number-one son of a man who truly did love and care. For one whole week, I wouldn't hear criticism. For one whole week, we could belong together, one happy family.

CHAPTER TWO

COME WITH ME

Like a Dog Chasing the Tail

...of a kid's just-launched kite, another March storm nipped at the rear end of our airplane, heavy with bodies and luggage. Barely escaping the next Minnesota blizzard, we lifted off a plow-cleared runway in a sea of snowdrifts. It was the perfect time to get out of town.

Sandwiched with barely an inch extra for elbows or knees, my housemate Chuck and I were airborne on a chartered, non-stop flight—Minneapolis to Honolulu. The flight posed a boring, endless span of clouds with occasional glimpses of a deep, blue-black ocean.

Ahh, but landing at Honolulu International Airport! Deplaning on an open-air causeway. OMG! Sudden and intoxicating sensory overload! Sunshine, the warm kind, striking my shoulders. Warm, gentle breezes caressing my face. Tropical scents—unidentifiable, mesmerizing. Already in those first moments, Hawaiian spears were piercing my heart.

Excited, eager, yes, but I had not been prepared for this mind-blowing welcome to the land of aloha.

Impatiently checked into a no-frills, third-floor room in Outrigger East Hotel on Ka'iulani Avenue, we would be awakened each morning at 6:00 a.m. to the *beeep, beeep, beeep* of the garbage truck, collecting the trash just below our window. But that first evening we hustled to meet and greet our new playground, Waikīkī. We strolled up Kūhiō Avenue toward Hamburger Mary's. Honolulu's gay nightlife was beckoning.

I had learned a bit about pronouncing Hawaiian. Sound out each and every letter. Vowel sounds are ah / ay / ee / oh / ooh. Ambling over each cross street, I began to sound out street names.

"Kah-ee-ooh-lah-nee."

"Kah-nee-kah-poh-lay."

"Wa-li-na."

"Nāhua."

"Nohonani."

Tears! Not just subtle moisture in my eyes. Tears, welling up and seeping softly onto my cheeks.

"Well, this is a new encounter!" I muttered under my breath. Confused by my intense, emotional reaction to Hawaiian words, I experienced my first clue. Hawai'i was more than a winter getaway vacation. But what, exactly?

During two weeks on O'ahu, Hawai'i seeped into my skin, won my heart, and made my soul her hostage. I enjoyed maximum daylight hours at Queen's Surf, Honolulu's unofficial gay beach. A flat grassy lawn, perfect for sunbathing, with the hypnotizing sway of palm trees framing an unimaginably blue sky. The endless *whoosh whoosh whoosh* of ocean waves collapsing onto the sandy beach. The sweetness of frozen fruit bars at the concession stand. The pungent aroma of gardenia, wafting on the gentle healing trade winds. And at predictable intervals, "Okay, I'm hot and sweaty again. Time for another plunge." Arise. Walk across warm grass onto the downward slope of sandy beach into seawater. Then dive forward and immerse body and heart and soul into the deep massaging coolness of the Pacific Ocean blue.

In the Photo

I am beaming into the camera with my red-framed glasses and wall-to-wall smile, holding a bright turquoise beach towel flapping ferociously *above* my head. Oh, the Pali wind!

For one day, we rented a car to drive around Oʻahu. The first stop for every tourist is Pali Lookout with its astounding view of the Windward side atop the Koʻolau mountain range. The trade winds slammed against a 3,000-foot wall after 2,500 miles of open ocean. Not an everyday experience in Minnesota.

Back into the rented car, up through the mid-island pineapple fields, we coasted into the sleepy town of Haleʻiwa. A quaint sight, this fading sugar plantation town had a sort of hippie flavor.

Halfway through town, Chuck spotted a storefront. "Matsumoto's Shave Ice! Let's stop."

So we did. A mom-and-pop shop, so prevalent in the islands, Matsumoto's was unique. It was a stand-out tourist destination. A dark, dingy interior belied the treat in store for us—Hawaiian shave ice. Likened to the mainland's crystalized snow cones, the two should not share the same sentence. Crafted by a rotating blade, which shaves a block of ice, the white snowflakes fill a paper cone. Result—a fine flaky delight, flavored with an array of sweet syrups. I ordered the tropical blend—yellow pineapple, orange mango, blue coconut. Yummmmmy!

From Hale'iwa, we ventured further along the North Shore. Eager to step bare feet into the water, we pulled off the highway and hustled down to the beach. An idea percolated in my brain.

"Chuck, you know the calendar I bought yesterday, Men of Hawai'i? Remember the chiseled hunk, crawling up out of the surf like some primordial god? Let's replicate it."

So we did. I went first. Chuck captured a fine parody of me, lifting myself on one arm, rising up out of the surging tide.

"Great! Now your turn." I took the camera and steadied, while Chuck lowered himself, ready to crawl out of the sea. "Okay, on three. One. Two…" A predictable surge wave swept ashore, submerging and overwhelming my friend. I shot a sequence of four photos—Chuck, gasping for breath, clambering up like a drowning rat. We laughed all the way to Kahuku.

Our Faces Suggest, Perhaps We Shouldn't Have

An accommodating hiker had taken the photo. Chuck and I leaning against a post, each of us held up by one arm, grasping the state sign, Kalalau Trail. Uncharacteristically slumped, my hair a tangled mop, legs and clothing mud stained. I'm a mess.

The morning prior, on our two-day side trip to Kaua'i, we had embarked on an excursion, "a moderately difficult hike of eleven miles from Ke'e Beach to Kalalau Valley on Kaua'i's north shore." At the trailhead, we learned that we needed a permit. A three-hour detour to Līhu'e and back, we left Ke'e Beach after noon. The trail was muddy and slippery. Rain alternated with sunshine alternated with rain alternated with sunshine alternated with rain… Six miles in with approaching sunset, we set up camp at Hanakoa Falls. Not a bad second choice, we swam with a 1,500-foot waterfall plunging into the far side of a pool. Pummeled by water off the cliff, the swim and bath were a refreshing reward for a day hike more challenging than we had anticipated.

The next morning, we lazed about, prolonging our idle pleasures in a setting pristine with beauty. Not eager to repeat the battle of the trail, we had no choice. One way in, same way out. We slipped more than stepped. Footing was precarious, demanding more focus and energy than any previous hike.

Arriving at Ke'e Beach in mid-afternoon, we asked a nearby hiker to take our photo. When the snapshot was developed, we agreed. "Yes, we really were that beaten down."

"Let's Go, Boy. Come with Me."

Grandpa Glasener beckoned me as he rose from his chair at the head of the table and set off for the door. I sprang to my feet and rushed behind the old man, who paused in the entry to don his cap, stained and odorous with countless hours of sweat.

I bounded eagerly along, alternating beside, behind, or ahead of him, trying to measure my pace to his. Walking with a familiar limping gait, Grandpa stoically endured the pain of a right knee which should have been, but never was, repaired. It was just the way Grandpa walked. At age eight, I never connected it with old age or pain or disability.

Excited, I tried to match his stride. Following Grandpa Glasener on a weekday morning down the drive from house to apple shed could only mean one thing. We were off to deliver freshly picked strawberries. A drive of fifty miles from Herbster, Wisconsin, to Superior and Duluth, delivery errands would consume a whole day. A whole day—just Grandpa and me! A boy can be so simply overjoyed.

The morning drive was uneventful yet memorable. With crates of strawberries loaded on the truck, we headed west. In the first few miles to Port Wing, the truck traveled close to the south shore. I could never tire of glimpsing through the trees to gaze across that mesmerizing Lake Superior. In the middle part of the drive, we passed through country of shrubbery and barely harvestable farm fields. Hugging the southern shoreline as we approached Superior, I gazed dreamily across the narrowing waters to Duluth and Minnesota's North Shore.

Routinely, Grandpa made his rounds, stopping at small markets in Superior and Duluth. Sometimes he told me to wait inside the truck. Other times he muttered a few words and bid me get out to help carry a crate into a market, where he introduced me as "my grandson Ric, best strawberry picker in Wisconsin." Wow, did I beam with pride!

On most days after hard work, Grandpa Glasener sat silently at the table, listening intently to the radio, especially the daily broadcast from Paul Harvey. I always hold the same image of my grandfather. He could pass as a double for the figure in that portrait "Grace," the painting of the old man sitting with hands raised and folded in prayer, which hangs in so many Midwestern homes.

At age eight, absolutely nothing could compete with a whole day spent with Grandpa Glasener. That could make a boy proud just to be.

Jolly Roger's Restaurant

Everything green except for the food—eggs, bacon, toast, and coffee—served promptly by green-clad friendly wait help. Open-air windows looking onto Kūhiō Avenue just around the corner from our hotel. Everything we needed to begin our day.

Morning one—all abuzz. Busy chatter across the table about what to do, when, and where.

Morning two—I was quiet. Didn't talk as much. Preoccupied with…thinking…

Morning three—I sat silent as I ate with my friend. My mind was away—drifting, struggling, reaching.

On morning four, I took a deep breath and blurted aloud, "Okay, I just have to say it out loud. Hawai'i is my home. I'm moving here."

CHAPTER THREE

ON NAMING

You Cannot Write About That!

We all recognize the voice of our inner disciplinarian. He/she/they issue commands. Discussion is not on the table. "Those thoughts are private—even secret. Never meant to be shared. You can't write about that!" My inner protector was having nothing to do with sharing a thing forever restricted, hush-hush.

"Oh, yeah?" Never one big on following orders, I rebutted. "My memoir coach Darien Gee quotes Frances Kakugawa. 'Be honest. Once you begin to censor your work because you're afraid of what others will say, you will lose the power of writing.'[2] Discussion closed."

My secret: I have a Hawaiian name.

Truth is, I have always been a bit embarrassed by my story. "I mean, really? Is that how it happened? Kinda strange, huh?" Add to my hesitancy, I have near-sacred respect for Hawaiian names and naming.

---

2. Darien Gee, *Writing the Hawai'i Memoir* (Watermark Publishing, 2014).

I know so many malihini who come to Hawai'i, adopt a Hawaiian name, and anoint themselves. That doesn't ring true for me. It borders on disrespect for Hawaiian culture.

In the early months of 1987 before moving from Minnesota to Honolulu, I was practicing a daily mind-conscious shamanic kind of meditation. Entering my inner Hawaiian garden (a sanctum I created in my mind), I asked and received guidance, direction, healing.

Passing one morning through my white arbor, covered with aromatic growth of *maile* (a native shrub with shiny fragrant leaves used for decorations and lei), I glided through a central courtyard, past my Tree of Life. Ascending several stone steps, I approached a flat, grassy platform.

I hesitated. I had never been here before. It felt somehow more sacred. Was I supposed to walk forward? Gathering my courage, I ventured one step.

A voice (from where?) called out a name. "Aa-" [inaudible syllable] "-*liko*!" The voice was calling me. Not so much calling, more like summoning me. I realized in the moment that I was being beckoned by name.

The moment was so dramatic and unexpected, it jolted me out of my meditation, back into my bedroom in my Minneapolis apartment. I scrambled across the room and pulled my brand-new Hawaiian dictionary off the shelf.

Liko—leaf bud; newly opened leaf; to bud; to put forth leaves. Fig., a child or descendant, especially of a chief; youth…Shining, glistening, as with dew; sparkling, glowing; burning.[3]

Wow! Cool! Did I love that! "I've been given a Hawaiian name!"

Later I learned that as a name, it is Kaliko. I hadn't discerned the *Ka-*.

In 1998, learning Hawaiian quilting from my Aunty Vi in Hilo, I discovered that she had been taught quilting as a young girl in Kalapana by her grandmother, Kaliko Ka'aukai. Aunty Vi called me her *hānai* (adopted) son. In my mind, I know. I am Kaliko, the hānai great-grandson of a Hawaiian woman named Kaliko Ka'aukai.

I never use my Hawaiian name. I hold it dear and sacred in my heart. Aunty Vi heard me tell this story. As often happened when I shared things spiritual, she sat silent, listening, nodding in knowing approval.

In my heart, I cradle that day in 1987 with sacred humility (*ha'aha'a*). Writing this today is the first time I have shared this story in any public way. If this story is included in my Hawai'i memoir, that will take more courage than I have on this day of penning it.

I am Kaliko. That's my name. That's part of my story.

---

3. Mary Kawena Pukui and Samuel Elbert, *Hawaiian Dictionary* (University of Hawai'i Press, 1986).

Ric Douglas Stark

Trust me, I didn't give myself that name, it's what my 1949 birth certificate says. Ric Stark. Too short. Too choppy. Who would choose such a name?

Names were the prerogative of my father. Never able to get a satisfactory explanation from my mom (she claimed Douglas was for the county name of Omaha, where I was born), I suspect Mom evaded the truth.

My dad named his sons after his current "best friends." Second son, Jeffory Bill was named after favored college friend Bill Ratten. Third son was named for another flame, Dick Draper. Yes, my younger brother is Richard. I could never lengthen my name. I always had to defend mine, "No, I'm Ric, no 'k.'"

I love long names. In earlier days when I dreamed of raising a family, I played with naming sons Jeremiah or Daniel or Zachary or my favorite, Nathaniel. One of my few regrets in life—never raising a child. One small part of that regret—never having the opportunity to name one.

"R-i-c"—no "k." That's my name. If I ever dared, I would love to be known as Kaliko. But that name is private, not for public consumption.

Is not loving my name linked to some deeper self-animus? I have never asked a therapist. I just sign, "Ric d. Stark". That's my name.

Chapter Four

PARADISE—FRESH OFF THE BOAT

Chuggg, Chugg, Chu...

Glancing at the dashboard, red light flashing, I groaned, "Nooooo! I'm out of gas!"

Just past the entrance ramp onto H-1, barely merged into mounting rush-hour traffic, I felt dread as my one-year-old Chevy Nova refused to comply with my foot as I stomped on the accelerator. I slowed, rolled, stopped—one wheel against the cement wall, the other halfway into traffic. Complicating my desperate situation, I was on a curve. Oncoming traffic didn't see me until too close for comfort.

Day five in my new home in Hawai'i, I had my car but *he pilikia* (trouble) had me. I had memorized the directions. Sand Island Road to Nimitz Highway (airport-bound) to H-1 (Honolulu-bound) to Pali Highway exit. Left on North School Street, back to the office at Comprehensive Home Services of Hawai'i. Piece of cake.

Like baking a cake in a flame oven, both endeavors require one crucial ingredient—gas. I had none. Shippers drain gas tanks to below one-eighth. I knew that. I hadn't noticed the red light on the gas gauge.

August 1987. Before cell phones. I flicked on my hazard lights, dashed across a gap in speeding traffic, and hiked four blocks to a gas station, heart pounding from panic and from exertion.

A half-hour later, distress call accomplished, I sat behind the wheel and spied the flashing red lights of a tow truck. A hefty local man assessed the situation and hooked me up for a tow.

Waiting inside my car, my frustration mounted and reached the boiling point. Everything about this move had been fraught with complications. I was struggling to find affordable housing. I had packed away important papers needed for vehicle registration. Shipping my belongings across the ocean, every piece of wooden furniture had splintered or broken. And I didn't yet have one friend who could comfort me. Distraught, furious, unbelieving, I sat pounding my arms on the steering wheel, screaming aloud, "WHY THE FUCK DID I DO THIS? TAKE ME HOME TO MINNESOTA!"

The driver frowned. I think he was seriously asking himself, "Am I safe to give this idiot a tow?"

That "why the f***" question plagued me during my first year in Hawai'i. Alone in a strange land, unaware of customs and protocols, lonely for companionship that was too slow in coming my way, fearful that I had made a terrible life choice, I often bemoaned to myself, "Why did I do this? Minnesota was so much easier!"

But often in life, the answer comes in a song and a dance.

Time to Cast Doubts Aside and Know the Wonder

"I'm here, Hawai'i, so let's get on with it! Show me your magic at last!"

It was the late '80s and, yes, I did love to dance. Disco was king—and queen—and I was a loyal subject. Never learning the hip, in-vogue moves, mine was the free-form dance style of a white boy—more esoteric, less groovy. But, man, did I love to dance disco, especially with a partner who loved it equally!

Who can sit still inside their bones when a Donna Summer song begins to play? My body hears the rhythm—I simply must start movin' 'n' groovin'!

Gay dancing in Honolulu in the late '80s meant Hula's. A bit more glam than her sister bar, Hamburger Mary's, Hula's featured a disco dance floor. Both bars were open-roofed. It rained so seldom at night in Waikīkī that simply wasn't a hindrance.

Point of reference—I hate bars. I have long and deep issues with alcohol. My father (the most functional alcoholic I've ever known) could hold his liquor. But I suffer the emotional scars of a typical adult child of an alcoholic. Encounter with an inebriated man in a gay bar? Not on my list! Not a smoker, I find little attraction with a smoke-filled bar. Added negative—I have never been able to hear well in a room filled with pounding music and a din of loud voices.

But the downsides of that noisy, crowded smoke-filled bar of near-drunks were not enough to dissuade me from my passion for kicking up my heels on Hula's dance floor. Captive to the allure, I devoted my weekends to Waikīkī. Baking in the sun at Queen's Surf by day and shaking my bones on the dance floor by night.

I'm not "bar pretty." While attractive enough, I never stood out in a gay bar, never made one friendship or partnership from any bar encounter. It's not Ric's thing. Today, I don't recall being inside a gay bar since 1988. It's just something that once was.

You Have a Gay Friend?

"Can I meet him?" I must have sounded too eager. "I'm curious."

A man way ahead of his time, Sam may be the least prejudiced person I've ever known. My gay curiosity didn't faze my straight classmate. I asked to meet Erik. Sam accommodated. Connections were made and the three of us decided to meet at a gay bar in downtown Minneapolis.

May 1976. Graduation from physical therapy school fast approaching, I was toying with arson and pretending not to notice. The kind of arson that would burn down my own carefully closeted life.

Outside the doors of The Gay 90's, Sam introduced me to Erik, a blond-blond, perfectly groomed with Nordic features. We shook hands and smiled. Covertly, I studied his face. He was wearing make-up. His face was smoothed with foundation. I could see eyeliner. He wore rouge on his cheeks.

Fidgeting, my hands would not remain still. Already bouncing to the faint sound of disco, my legs complained of the delay. My eyes kept shifting to the flashing marquee, The Gay 90's. Reading my anticipation, Erik gestured, "Shall we?"

We strolled toward the door, past the bouncer, and I was immediately bombarded with music blasting. "That's Where the Happy People Go" by the Tramps cranked full blast. It was a Tuesday night, yet the club was packed. An antique bar dominated the far wall. Lights flickered and a rotating disco ball pulsed with the music. Glasses of liquor, the haze of cigarette smoke. Everywhere I looked, I saw mirrors.

But men—everywhere, men. Men together. Men laughing. Men drinking and talking. Men standing together—close. Men touching one another—couples holding hands, embracing, kissing. Men dancing together, some shirtless, unafraid to bump or grind their bodies against one another. Men celebrating life and joy and just being themselves. Together.

I entered that bar, a man two years married. My wife, Ginny, and I were currently trying to get pregnant. I was a son and grandson with a rebellious streak, for sure, but was I queer? God, no! I was an almost-graduated physical therapist, a jock with a job. But was I a faggot, a guy who liked guys? I tried for so long not to think so. But already I was wondering— who would be the man coming out of that bar?

The world—my world—might never understand how it had taken less than a minute for me to realize—this was home. This was where I belonged.

When I left the bar later that evening, I was still the same man. Still married to my wife, still the rebellious son of a proud, decent, preacher man, still an almost-graduated physical therapist. But a man with a newfound identity—a man who is gay. The Gay 90's was the first of many places where Ric could be Ric. Proud and joy-full and gay.

CHAPTER FIVE

E KOMO MAI—WELCOME

Crrreeeeek. Drmmm. Drmmm. Drmmm. Vrrrroooooooom!

Brakes. Idle. Gas!

When I moved to O'ahu, I rented a house in a quiet neighborhood on a side street in Kāne'ohe town. Or so I thought. My quiet side street was part of a shortcut, which enabled local Kāne'ohe traffic to avoid a ten-minute wait for commuters to crawl through stop lights onto Likelike Highway, headed into Honolulu. Third house from the corner, between 5:00 to 9:00 a.m. those sounds were my morning alarm clock.

But my noisy morning wake-up call rewarded me. Motivated to rise early and head to one of my favorite spots, I often greeted sunrise at nearby Ulupō Heiau in the midst of "church row" into Kailua. Practicing a spiritual tradition of Hawaiian shamanism, I accomplished daily meditations of inner shamanic journeys and quests.

My favorite place to meditate was Ulupō. Bordering Kawainui Marsh with a view spanning from the Pacific to the Ko'olau Range, this Hawaiian temple held an aura heightened during dawn or dusk. Ulupō held vibrational energy of the mystical. Not an accident, the name Ulupō: *"Ulu"* means "to grow, to increase." *"Pō,"* meaning "night," refers to the underworld, the spirit world. Repeatedly when I meditated at Ulupō, I transported to a place and experience that became so vivid, so surreal, that it felt like I was traveling in time and space, not simply meditating on a *pōhaku* (stone) beside the swamp in Kailua, Hawai'i.

Another thing happened to me at Ulupō—I frequently encountered *pueo*, the Hawaiian owl, flying above me across the *heiau*. One evening deep into a meditative state, I had passed well into the dream world, leaving behind me the pōhaku where I sat. A piercing shriek jolted me out of my meditation. Startled and frightened, I leapt to my feet and gazed upward. There was a pueo, hovering no more than thirty feet above my head. In a few seconds, he swooped off toward the swamp and disappeared into the trees.

No need to ask a *kahuna* (priest). I knew that I had identified my *'aumakua,* the Hawaiian term for family god or guardian spirit. Through the years, I see pueo. When I'm contemplating a big decision, pueo will fly across my path or sit, alert but silent, on a fence post or a bare branch. Meaningful, reassuring, and nurturing as my personal spirit guide, pueo validates my decision-making. He affirms my life path, made with deliberate and hard-won choosing. Always, I am grateful.

How Would I Fare in the Home of an Island Native?

Queasy. Exiting H-1, turning left on Coyne Street, I spied the address number on the second house—my first home-health client.

A thirty-something woman appeared and inquired, "You must be Rick? Come in. I'm Josie, Frances's daughter."

"Yes, I am Ric, the physical therapist from Comprehensive Home Services," I answered as I stooped to untie and slip off my shoes. Forewarned at the office, I knew that local style was to remove our shoes before entering someone's home.

Inside a bedroom, I met Frances, a woman of Hawaiian-Portuguese ancestry. With tired but friendly eyes, she greeted me and gestured for me to sit in a chair, pulled near the bed. Illness and fatigue did nothing to dampen Island manners of hospitality.

I began. "I understand you've just come home yesterday from a week-long stay at Queen's. How are you doing, Mrs. Sanchez?"

"Oh, you can call me Frances. I'm fine. A little bit weak, but I'm getting better now."

I was immediately captivated by this woman's warm, heartfelt spirit. Over time I would learn that Frances Sanchez was a rare pure example of the warm and genuinely welcoming, loving personality that we call "the spirit of aloha."

I directed our conversation to my evaluation of her physical abilities and needs. Could she get up and down from bed? Did she need help to walk? Was Josie needing to assist her with dressing and help her in the bathroom? I was drawing on all my skills as a physical therapist and applying them to learning the needs of this woman in her own home.

But Frances had different priorities. "So where do you come from? And what brings you to our beloved Hawai'i?"

I chuckled and blushed. "Here I'm trying so hard to do everything right and to fit in. I don't know the Island customs, especially with so many people from different cultures. And you realized in a minute that I'm brand new. What do you call it? FOB? Fresh off da boat?"

We laughed together. "You don't need to worry about any of that, Ric. As long as you treat people with respect and have aloha in your heart, you will be just fine. Oh, and always remember to remove your shoes at the door."

A special rapport had been born so easily. I worked with Frances Sanchez for five or six weeks. On our last visit, I made a special point to thank her. "You have been the perfect first client to greet me in Hawai'i. You made me feel comfortable and welcome—in your home and in Hawai'i. *Mahalo nui loa*." We hugged and she kissed my cheek, both of us a bit misty-eyed.

It Didn't Take That Long

But it took longer than I had patience.

"God, please allow me a friend in this strange land."

Attending Unity Church in Kailua, I took a weekend seminar that Therese Godfrey taught on "prosperity consciousness," all the thing in the '80s. The universe is one of limitless potential and supply and God wants us to enjoy bounty. "Lack" is a thing we create in our own limited thinking, not something natural or God-appointed.

Therese and I became buddies during her course that fall in 1987. Sharing frequent morning walks along Kailua Bay, we occasionally hiked together for an afternoon on a mountain trail.

Our friendship cemented over Thanksgiving. For several years, Therese spearheaded a community dinner in Kailua—turkey dinners and fellowship for all who showed up. A half-dozen volunteers offered to assist. I don't remember what the crisis was, but something had gone awry and the dinner itself was in doubt. At 8:30 a.m., we joined hands in a circle and invoked help from above.

Whatever the flashpoint, it abated. Serving some 125 meals to a grateful gathering of folks in the community, dinner was a raving success. It even made the evening news.

The outcome—Therese and I were solid friends for life. That day began a decade-long tradition. Wherever we lived, Therese and I shared Thanksgiving dinner together until she moved to Georgia to care for her aging mother in the late 1990s.

CHAPTER SIX

NOT SO FAST

How Much Sun Can a White Man Endure?

In Minnesota, three months full on—June, July, August. In Hawai'i? Let's find out.

I moved to Hawai'i in 1987 in answer to a relentless, spiritual calling. Hawaiian language stirred my soul. Her music—more so. I read about Hawai'i, meditated on Hawai'i, dreamt of Hawai'i. I had been given a Hawaiian name. Hawai'i nestled and made home in my heart. She called, I answered.

Alongside the call of spirit, a short list of perks—sun, beach, no winters, no snakes. In Minnesota, I revered my brief summer sun-basking. I prized my golden tan, always with its underlying tinge of red. Now in Hawai'i, I could bask in year-round beach time.

For the first year, I did just that. Queen's Surf became my weekend hangout. Named for Queen Lili'uokalani, who had a beach house in the area, the stretch of beach on the Diamond Head end of Waikīkī had been unofficially adopted by the gay community.

Affording a sprawling lawn with towering swaying coconut palms, a sloping white sand beach, a gentle ocean swim inside the reef, and a concession stand with facilities, Queen's Surf provided a hospitable gathering place for Honolulu's gay men and a few lesbians.

Living across the Koʻolau, I preferred the company of my own gay people over the straight family crowds at Kailua Beach. Arriving late morning, I baked in the Hawaiʻi sun for long afternoons. A couple of times each hour, heat and sweat would necessitate a saunter across the beach for a cool refreshing plunge into the ocean. Rejuvenated, I was afforded the ever-inviting opportunity to stroll the beach, alert for the inviting stare and smile of a potential "friend."

The first summer of 1988, I experienced a complication. Reacting to Hawaiʻi's intense sun on my sensitive, Caucasian skin, I developed a rash. My chest broke out with something akin to pimples. They were sore. It hurt. Increasing the SPF in my suntan lotion, I developed an allergic reaction to coconut oil.

I could no longer ignore decades of medical advice. The sun's UV rays were not healthy—especially not for this haole guy in the tropics—so my sun-and-beach days ended. For thirty-plus years now, I go to the beach only before 10:00 a.m. or after 4:00 p.m. The scent of coconut oil makes my stomach turn.

Much to Learn

So many different peoples, cultures, customs. Where to begin?

Moving to Hawaiʻi and living in Hawaiʻi were not easy. Running out of gas on the freeway two minutes after retrieving my car from Matson shipping. Being cited with a parking ticket for an unregistered vehicle but lacking my car registration papers to correct the offense since the papers were in my belongings on the slow boat. The impossibility of dealing with the state government—it took multiple trips and a month to navigate the requirements of the Department of Motor Vehicles. Those were just the logistical challenges, saying nothing of my landing alone in a strangers' land. Too many cultures, too many pidgin words landing on my clueless ears. Too many foods I wanted to taste but didn't comprehend. Too many lonely days and nights before I grew friendships.

During my first year, I struggled fiercely—financially, socially, emotionally. Drawn to Hawaiʻi by a compelling, powerful, spiritual force, I knew that I was called to be here. In the year-long gap between my first vacation and final landing, I thought, heard, listened to music, sang, danced, and dreamed Hawaiʻi. I *had* to come!

But knowing that calling and realizing true belonging were two disparate matters. Early on I had adopted my own personal motto, "I did not move to Hawaiʻi to live in haole heaven." My early experiences often punched me with a forceful reply, "You jus' one mo' haole from da mainland."

Enchanted with Hawaiian Words

I wanted to learn the Hawaiian language. In autumn 1987, I searched and found an evening adult-extension class offered by Kamehameha Schools. Joining a class of twenty-five adults, there may have been one or two other white folks, but the class was predominantly comprised of locals.

An older man with a compelling presence introduced himself as the teacher and explained he had grown up on Hawai'i Island (also called the Big Island) in a home of native speakers. He was one of the last—a *kanaka maoli*, a native-born person who spoke Hawaiian as a native tongue, not as a learned or second language.

All engines, go! I was eager and excited to learn. In the second week, I raised my hand to clarify a puzzling question.

"Yes? You have a question?" He acknowledged me.

"Yes, sir, mahalo. Can you please explain the 'e' sound? When you say the word 'Pele,' I hear two different 'e' sounds."

"No, they are the same. Pele." He was curt.

I persisted. "Okay, but I hear the first 'e' as a short 'eh' and the second 'e' as a long 'eee.'"

The professor swept his eyes across the room and addressed the class. "See? That's the problem with people who come to Hawai'i to 'learn' our language. They don't belong among us. And they think we should explain what we are saying to them."

He persisted with words I do not recall. I shriveled in my chair. I felt like a squashed cockroach—unclean, unwanted, undeserving. I sat numb for the remainder of class, then rushed from the room, never to return.

Thirty-four years later that one still hurts my heart. I came to Hawai'i with such eager enthusiasm. I wanted to embrace my new culture. What better way than to learn her language, her *'ōlelo*? To be rebuffed so unkindly and so publicly—and by a teacher of that culture—was an early humiliation. I returned to the Hawaiian language with different teachers in different classrooms. But that first encounter sounded a warning.

Belonging in Hawai'i would not be a cakewalk.

CHAPTER SEVEN

MEETING MADAME PELE

What's a Big Island Adventure Without a Little Risk?

We agreed. In October 1988, the Saddle Road between Hilo and Kona had stretches that were nearly four-wheel-drive. Rental companies refused to accept any liability for damage or breakdowns on Saddle Road.

My friend Chuck, visiting from Minnesota (yes, the same Chuck from fourteen nights in Waikīkī for $550), joined me for my first visit to the Big Island. My first trip to Madame Pele's home turf.

Defying our car rental contract, we camped our first two nights in sparsely equipped cabins at Pōhakuloa. Situated mid-point on Saddle Road at 6,500-foot elevation, our cabin afforded stunning beauty, peace, and quiet. For two nights, we were companioned by nothing but the gusting winds, which swooped across the gap between Mauna Kea and Mauna Loa.

Quiet lazy hours, we lounged at Pōhakuloa. The mornings especially! So cold—chilly even under the thin, wool blankets. We popped out of our beds and started moving around at sunrise just to warm our fingers and cheeks.

The next three days were plotted across the island at Nāmakanipaio in Volcanoes National Park. Just off Māmalahoa Belt Highway, one mile from the park entrance, the campground announced itself loudly. It was so busy and noisy after the isolation of Pōhakuloa. Settling in, we pulled out our visitors' guide map of the park.

We scheduled our time ahead:

Day One—morning hike across the crater to Halemaʻumaʻu.

Night One—drive down Chain of Craters Road to view the lava flows.

Day Two—drive up Mauna Loa Access Road and hike in Kīpuka Puaulu.

Night Two—dinner at Volcano House, overlooking the crater.

Day Three—drive back to Kona; Aloha Airlines back to Honolulu.

Our itinerary was all set. My eyes, mind, heart, soul were ill-prepared for the coming encounters. I had no idea how the next few days would impact my future life in Hawai'i.

Lavish Abundance of Disparate Terrain

Planet Earth astounds, yet few landscapes are so unearthly as Kīlauea Crater, home of Hawaiian goddess Pele.

Our first morning in Volcano, Chuck and I hiked a trail down from the rim of Kīlauea Crater, descending through the rainforest, then out across twisting arms of *pāhoehoe* lava. With giant furrows of smooth, intertwining lava stone, it was as if we were traversing a freshly plowed field of some giant goddess. Our mile-plus hike brought us to the brim of Halemaʻumaʻu. Standing on the roped-off lookout, I gazed in wonder down several hundred feet into the heart of the abode of Madame Pele, the Hawaiian goddess called "she who shapes the sacred land." Plumes of yellow sulfur gas pulsed from vents in the lava. Hues of yellows, grays, browns, and oranges wrestled with one another to dominate a color impression. *Koaʻe* (white-tailed tropicbirds) soared overhead. I had never witnessed anything so unlike planet Earth—it was a landscape not imagined even in an alien world. The morning hike created an eerie mood, tilting my mind toward the bizarre.

Unsettled by an inundation of our senses, we returned to our cabin near noon, grabbed a quick lunch, packed our day packs with water and flashlights, and headed out on Chain of Craters Road from the volcano summit down to the ocean. At the road's dead end, we parked along the roadside among the hundred or so cars belonging to tourists like us, eager to glimpse lava from a real live volcano.

The lava flow had shifted to the southern edge of the five-year continuous flow. Conditions were unique, such that park rangers supervised visitors approaching the very fingers of new lava flow. Standing no more than ten to twenty feet distant, we watched pools of searing lava ooze from the rock.

A puddle would swell and flow, then stabilize and harden into black pāhoehoe rock. Molten red-hot liquidity hardened to black stone right before our eyes in less than one minute. Seconds later another pocket would swell and emit a new finger of sizzling-hot lava. Like watching cake batter being poured into a pan, lava flowed and rippled as it surged forth, then solidified into black pōhaku.

We took turns kneeling and posing for a picture. I hollered, "Chuck, take the picture!" Kneeling some four feet from the red lava, my backside was cooking in just those few seconds.

Amazing Experiences

Niagara Falls, Grand Canyon, Yosemite, Kīlauea Crater. When visiting Earth's awe-inspiring wonders, we plan and prepare ourselves for them. But the off-the-scale encounters—these catch us unknowing, unready.

Late afternoon, Chuck and I set off to return to our car, get our gear, and find an ideal spot to sit and await darkness. We were promised an amazing show, viewing the night lava as it coursed down the mountain into the sea.

Somehow, we got off the main unmarked trail. No problem. The ocean was directly below us, so we simply headed in the direction of the pulsing sea. The road and our car lay ahead.

Traipsing around a steep lava wall, we lurched to a halt. We halted and gaped. Before us stood an embankment, perhaps ten feet high and thirty or forty feet long. Encased in the lava, faces—dozens of human faces returned our stares. Etched into the stone, a sculpture that no human artist could have carved with more presence. Chuck and I shot glances at one another. "Are you seeing…?" "Faces, yes…" We were peering at a wall of human heads, carved into the stone by Madame Pele herself. Some were caught in sadness, others with an expression of terror. Most simply gawked with mouths open wide in a moment of "Oh-h-h!" They were caught in a startle, as unaware as we were of this sudden, unexpected encounter.

Seconds, minutes, half of an hour—time quit on us. Mute and unable to stir, we gazed in silence. When eventually released from our trance, we hurried away toward the road. Too weird, too unsettling to remain. Somehow, we knew we had encountered something off the scale of normal experience. And we had not been invited. No malice or injurious intent, we simply were not intended to be in that place.

When we reached the road, we approached the park rangers' trailer. When we explained our encounter, the rangers were puzzled. No one had seen or reported any such formation before. Turning and pointing to direct them, I wanted to lead them back to share the sight. I could not. No bearings or direction, it was as though a portal had opened briefly, allowing us entrance into something not quite permitted. Just as quickly, we had been ushered out and away and the hatch closed and clicked behind us.

It was one of the weirdest experiences of my seventy-one years of life. I have revisited the memory so many times, I have searched for reason and purpose. I have asked for understanding. Nothing comes to me.

On a sunny afternoon in 1988, I encountered a sculpture of human faces, carved into a wall of pōhaku by Madame Pele in her lava flow near the ocean. That's all I know. I wish it had meaning and a message. It does not.

I came. I saw. I left.

I remember.

My Earliest Memory

Sunday school—I am four years old. A circle of chairs with eight to ten boys and girls, sitting in a basement room of the Hudson Community Church in Hudson, Iowa. A tall, black piano against the wall. An older woman, whom Mom will later identify as Ruth Strayer. Mrs. Strayer is at the piano, playing a tune and teaching us to sing "Jesus Loves Me."

I have poor and limited musical memory. All my life I have enjoyed a wide variety of musical genres and artists, yet I can hum only a few tunes and name even fewer artists with their song titles. For example, Joni Mitchell sang something about paradise in a parking lot. Neil Young sang about his old man being a lot like him. That's about it. Weird, right?

So today, if you were to ask me to sing a song that I remember, odds are you will hear me sing, "Jesus loves me. This I know. For the Bible tells me so…"

But years later in my forties, I learned that Sunday school was not my first memory. I have two earlier, vivid memories stored away.

This first is at the community park in Hudson, Iowa. It is the annual Hudson Easter egg hunt. All the town's kids are gathered here—parents stand nearby to root and cheer. On cue, the mob launches in all directions, hunting and gathering Easter eggs in the park.

I hold my little basket, walking and searching for colored eggs. I spy an egg, run toward it, only to have another kid rush in and snatch the egg before I do. This happens a few times. I begin to cry. Then Grandma Stark steps up, reaches out, and slaps a kid's hand. "Hey! You leave that egg alone. That's Ricky's egg!"

I grab it. "I got an Easter egg!"

Mom was taken aback by that story. "Ric, how could you remember that? You were only two-and-a-half years old."

The other memory is in Peoria, Illinois. I am hoisted up on top of Uncle Russel's shoulders, a full head above a crowded span of heads. A train passes. I see Ike, waving from the railing of the caboose of his presidential car. Clinging desperately to Uncle Russel's head, I unclasp one hand and wave. "Mommy! There's Ike!"

When I shared this memory, Mom was stunned again. "Ric, you were two years old!"

Isn't the human mind a wonder? Our capacity for memory—what an amazing gift! With memory, we learn, we grow, we accomplish, we excel. Through memory, we discover treasures to hold dear and to love—the seeds of our spirit of aloha. Memory of the past teaches us what we need to live today in joy. Memory guides us into promises of tomorrow.

And the greatest gift is this. We treasure our memories—past, present, and future. Yet all of our memories answer to our beckoning right in this moment. Memory is now—forever now. Always. In all ways.

Ric with his mom, Marge Stark. Hui Kapa 'Apana o Waimea quilt show, 2007.

CHAPTER EIGHT

THE POWER OF WORDS

Haole Boy Here

"Yeah, I'm just one more haole boy." That's how I identified myself during my first decade in Hawai'i. Spoken with a chuckle, this defensive prop became my off-handed way of dismissing my foreigner status, while at the same time, subtly claiming, "Hey, I jus' like you— almos.'"

During those early years, there was always a struggle. I had answered such a powerful, spiritual summoning to make Hawai'i my home. I wanted so vehemently to belong to Hawai'i—to belong *in* Hawai'i.

My physical being sharply contradicts any wish of "being Hawaiian." With ash-blond hair, blue eyes, and pale pinkish skin, I could never attempt to "pass." My mannerisms are definitely Caucasian. In education, culture, and socioeconomic background, I am entirely white.

But to be Hawaiian—I did try. Working as a home health physical therapist, I learned and spoke pidgin. Pretty good at it, I was often greeted at a client's doorstep by an astonished family member, "Oh, we thought you were local when we talked to you on the phone."

And, yes, I live forever tasting the bitter flipside of being haole. Not often, but always too frequently, I hear the jeer uttered at my back. Walking away from a group of locals, usually men, something I have done or said prods their prejudices. "Ahhh, what a f***in' haole!"

"Ouch!" It always stings, striking a sensitive nerve. That saying, "Sticks and stones can hurt my bones, but words can never touch me"? So wrong! It wounds me every time, even after thirty-four years. I comprehend the misunderstanding. But it still hurts to be dismissed and castigated with one sharp utterance, "Jus' one mo' haole!"

I retort in my mind. "Don't let the unkind words injure. They speak from their own prejudice and misunderstanding. Don't buy what they sell." White man—yes. Different skin, different background— you bet. But "jus' one mo' f***in' haole"? Hell, no—I one Hawaiian-at-heart.

Being called to Hawai'i and answering that calling—I've mastered that one. Belonging in Hawai'i—that's a lifelong journey and voyage.

Hawaiian Words Have Meaning

Take the word "haole." "*Hā*" means "breath." "'*Ole*" is an adjective that connotes negative, "not." Literally, "haole" means "without breath."

Missionaries arrived in Hawai'i in 1820, filled with fervor and determination to convert the heathen. They viewed Hawaiians as a people who lacked the enlightened message of the gospel of the Christian faith.

For Hawaiians at the time of Western contact, there was no formalized religion—the gods were everywhere. Prayer was part of every daily activity. Spiritual counsel and communion with the gods were an integral part of life.

Hawaiians offered prayer in everything they did. Hā was an intrinsic element of every prayer. To offer prayer you stood, you prayed, you breathed deeply, you lifted your arms to the heavens, you blew a full exhale to send your prayer offering upward toward your god.

But Hawaiians observed the Christian missionaries praying so differently. They knelt, bowed their heads, closed their eyes, clasped their hands tightly, muttered or prayed in silence. They prayed inwardly without offering their prayers upward toward the God they summoned. White Christians prayed *hā 'ole*, without breath.

As time passed and culture evolved in Hawai'i, these Christians became the powerful and dominant race. Everything turned upside down in the eyes of native Hawaiians. Whites—they ruled the government, owned the land, held the power. But these people, who had come with their intentions of converting and saving the heathen natives, never learned to practice prayer as an integrated part of daily life.

They came to be known as haole. And it was NOT a compliment!

At Age Twelve, I Idolized My Grandpa Glasener

He was everything I aspired to become. During that year, I shared a private meeting with my family pastor, Dr. Derenfield, and announced my intention to become a Presbyterian minister. I remember my aim in life—to become like Jesus, as pure and holy as I could be. For me, Grandpa Glasener came as close as anyone I knew for providing me with that role model.

Grandpa was a stark contrast with my father. Dad smoked; Grandpa didn't. Dad drank; Grandpa scorned alcohol. Dad cursed; Grandpa never uttered a word of profanity. Dad told little white lies; not my grandfather. Dad was a sinner; Grandpa was a devout pious man of God.

I held my Grandpa Glasener on a high pedestal. Spending my summers with my grandparents in Herbster, Wisconsin, I immersed myself in the joy of living and being near him. Laboring long days, picking strawberries in the field, I yearned for Grandpa's pat on a shoulder and his word of approval. Laboring to pick the most berries, I could never match Uncle Dale, but I always equaled Aunt Alice Mae.

I dearly loved that old man. Years later, I memorized his grace, which he recited before each meal:

Our dear heavenly Faaatherrr,
We do thank you for this daaay,
For this liiife,

For the many blessings of this liiife.
We thank you for this foood
And the hands that have prepaaared it.
We ask you to watch ooover us and keeep us
Now and forever morrre.

I loved that drawl, the way he prolonged a word of each line. A man of God. That's what Grandpa Glasener was. That's what I aspired to become.

. . .

When I speak Grandpa's grace at a meal today, I connect intuitively with this "man of God." The words and the accent of the Iowan, farmer of the land, resonate and unite with the Hawaiian, farmer of the sea. Two peoples of two lands with different cultures—but all one same heart.

CHAPTER NINE
INTERSPECIES BONDS

The Absolute Love of My Life

My blue Chow Chow, Aka, Hawaiian for "shadow." Unequivocally my moment of greatest regret in life—the day I gave Aka away.

Between 1995 and 2003, Aka and I shared a unique interspecies bond. Purchased in Puna on Hawai'i Island when she was eight weeks old, the fluffy ball of fur rode home that evening, cupped in my lap. By the time we arrived in Volcano, the tiny puppy had bonded to me. I was her protector and comforter, a role which later flipped. Aka always wanted to ride on my lap, head out the window, facing the on-rushing wind as we sped forward. As she grew, never realizing her change in size, she climbed onto Papa's lap, unaware that her sixty-pound body spanned both my legs or that her bundle of fur blocked my view. For Aka, Papa's lap was where she belonged.

When she was six months old, we enrolled in puppy obedience class. From the first exercises, I marveled at Aka's attention and response to command. While the other puppies were distracted and lunged on their leashes, Aka kept glancing up at me, intent on answering my next command. By the third class, she anticipated and kept pace the instant I issued a new command or stepped in a different direction. Amazed at her performance, I lavished her with praise. I was so proud of my doggy, and our bond tightened and deepened.

Graduating puppy class, we began training for her obedience title. AKC-registered dogs perform feats of sit, down, come, heel, stay—both on- and off-leash. Performing in a ring before a judge, a dog must score 170-plus out of 200 points on three separate trials to receive the official commendation, "obedience dog."

In her final trial, she scored second place with 192½ points. When a judge in Hilo presented Aka with her degree, he commented, "I have only awarded obedience title to one other Chow. To earn this at age eighteen months is a remarkable achievement."

"Thank you," I beamed. "But the credit all belongs to Aka. She's just a special being."

And so she was. I have delighted in many dear and intimate relationships with deep bonds of love and mutual sharing, but Aka read me like no one ever has done. Cueing into the nonverbals, she headed for the door before I reached for car keys or uttered a word. Our best simple joy—hours shared tossing and retrieving her favorite, a tennis ball. Whenever I was troubled or saddened, I don't know how but always, there she was, curling up beside me to comfort and reassure. Inseparable. In sync. In love.

That bond and our communion created a painful irony in my mind. When she was nine years old, I answered a "calling from God" to enter a contemplative Episcopalian monastery in Wisconsin. Uninvited to live a prayer life, even though blue Chow Chows are considered sacred beings in Tibet, Aka was surrendered to my former partner Henry, an act for which I have yet to forgive myself.

Strange, that the dearest and most spiritual bond I ever shared with another was the one between a furry, blue Chow Chow and her grateful Papa. Equally bizarre that I willingly severed that bond and gave her away.

Aka, Ric's blue Chow Chow

I Have No Memory of Receiving My First Puppy

Scooter, my Boston Terrier, was a Christmas present from Santa Claus when I was five months old.

Growing up together, all of the early photographs of Ricky have Scooter right alongside. I reminisce of a snapshot of me sitting in my red wagon, sporting a new outfit with a favorite shirt printed with pink flamingos and a pair of shorts with suspenders. Scooter standing right in front of me, both of us smiling into the camera.

At age two—still an only child and first grandchild—the whole world was about Ricky and his best pal. Soon I had one brother, then another. My dominion made room for siblings, even as my world expanded to include friends and school. Of course, I had to share Scooter with my brothers, but he was always "Ricky's dog."

Seven years old. Our family drove to Uncle Bill and Aunt Natalie's farm on Eldora Road, five miles outside of Hudson, Iowa. The Glasener family was gathering for a celebration. It might have been my birthday.

I was eager to run inside. Grandma Glasener was always thrilled to see me, to let me know I was her special boy. Grandpa never said but I knew, even at age seven, that I was one of his favorites. I paid no attention as I threw open the car door and bounded out—Scooter jumping down behind me and running off across the lawn.

Inside Aunt Natalie's kitchen, I was laughing, sharing warm hugs and greetings. Suddenly, shrill voices filled the air—I heard Mommy screaming. Racing out the back door, I found my uncle fetching a dog from underneath our blue-and-white '55 Chevy. My doggy was one mass of red blood and raw flesh. Mistaking black and white Scooter for a stray pig, Uncle Bill's herding dog had attacked and torn Scooter, rending a gaping wound along one entire side of my pup.

Dad rushed Scooter to the vet, who tried to sew him up. He lingered for two days in pain and misery. Refusing to leave his side, I slept on the floor beside him. On the second day, the dog stopped breathing. Mommy had to break the news. Scooter was dead.

I cried for days. Inconsolable and refusing to eat, I lay on my bed, rebuffing pleas to get up or come outside. On day two, Grandpa Mether, the family's upstairs landlord of our rented house in La Porte City, Iowa, came into my bedroom and talked with me. Together we carried Scooter out into the field at the far end of the lot. Grandpa Mether dug a hole with a shovel. We wrapped Scooter in a blanket, laid my doggy down, and buried him.

I was able to bury my tears with Scooter. But today, some sixty-four years later, gentle tears are falling as I recall the memory of my first loss.

CHAPTER TEN

HUNTING FOR A RELATIONSHIP

The 1991 Governor's Award for Manufacturer of the Year Is Awarded to...

Carol Pregill, president of Hawai'i's garment industry association, paused for dramatic effect. "Henry Daniel for Hawaiian Heritage by Henry Daniel."

The banquet hall erupted into cheers of applause. Mother-daughter competitors sitting next to us stiffened. One daughter emitted an audible gasp of dismay. Henry's mom and sisters hooted cheers over the accolades. Henry sat stunned in his seat, so I prodded him to his feet.

At the podium, Henry spoke words of appreciation. I stepped forward to add, "We owe special gratitude to the family, especially to Henry's mom, Peggy. We couldn't have done this without her." The room echoed with chuckles. We had not prepared our remarks.

From its earliest beginnings, the relationship between Henry Daniel Kim and me was as much about our clothing manufacturing business as it was about romance and love. Married to our business, not one another, Henry and I were inseparable during the years 1988 through 2000. We lived together, ate together, slept together, worked together, created fetching clothing together, bought a home together, raised two dogs, one cat, two lovebirds, and seventeen chickens together. It was 24/7 for twelve years.

So what part of us was Ric and Henry? And what part of us was Hawaiian Heritage by Henry Daniel? I doubt any therapist could dissect it. Those years were a mania of drive and commitment. Thankfully they came during our forties. We would never have committed earlier nor had the energy in later years.

At our zenith of success with nearly one million dollars in sales in 1991, we were successful Hawai'i retailers in 1992 when Kmart opened the first mainland box store on Nimitz Highway. Wearing Henry's business suit design, Miss America Carolyn Sapp greeted customers on opening day. Standing nearby, Henry and I looked on, proud. Proud of Carolyn. Proud of Hawaiian Heritage. Proud of Hawai'i's successes.

That day foreshadowed our slow decline and doom. As mainland chain stores steadily invaded Hawai'i's long-isolated retail market, small local businesses were choked. There was simply no way we could compete when our cheapest women's outfit cost $35 to manufacture and Kmart was selling a ready-to-wear dress for $30. The chokehold gripped us slowly but inevitably. In a 2000 bankruptcy, we lost our home, our cars, and our business. The personal split came in a sudden dramatic event.

It has taken time to recover from the loss and disappointment of the dream venture. Twenty years later, I realize the gifts of those years:

Ric as artist.

Ric as creative spirit.

Ric as the man with patient tenacity to sew 400,000 hand stitches to give birth to a Hawaiian quilt.

Ric as the man with the vision and persistence to pen 150 micro memoirs on his path toward creating a magnum opus.

I have learned one lesson in life. The pivotally important revelations and self-discoveries in life may not come easily. These gifts are the reward of years of honest effort and hard labor. That's fitting—as it should be.

Contra Dancing!

How do you put one hundred gay men in a room and force them to get over the perpetual dilemma of who is or isn't pretty enough to ask to dance?

Summer 1985, a group of bluegrass musicians in Minneapolis initiated a unique tradition—weekly Friday evening line dancing for gays and lesbians (and their friends). Differing from square dance where the majority of moves are performed with one partner, in contra dancing, you begin with a partner, then step forward or backward to repeat the dance with a new partner. Well suited for the intended audience, some 75 to 100 participants joined the weekly frivolity.

I had been dancing a couple of months and enjoying the social gathering, a welcome alternative to smoky drunken gay bar crowds. Finishing an early dance, I walked off the floor and surveyed the room. There he was, leaning against the far wall. A tall lanky man with a beautiful suntan and a pleasant, inviting face. Handsome didn't come close—not to my eyes.

Well, the worst thing that can happen, I told myself, *is that he says, "No thanks."* But he didn't.

"Hi, I'm Ric. Care to join me for the next dance?"

"Sure. I'm Paul." Handshake firm and warm. Eyes bouncy and engaging. And, boy, did we have a good time that evening!

Fast forwarding, Paul Kessler and Ric Stark became a hot item during that next year. In all my relationships over the years, I have never known the same pairing of compatible sexual energy. Hooking up once a week for one long energetic night, we achieved excess exercise and little sleep.

The conflict was on the emotional level. Sexual compatibility—100 percent. Emotional match—minus 10 percent. I was all in and burned for a relationship with Paul. But while Paul was all in on the sex, he was "all out" on any romantic relationship. Wrong timing? Wrong personality matches? Wrong life goals? I will never know.

I moved to Hawai'i. Paul moved to New England to live a half-dozen years off the grid in Vermont. After some twenty years, we reconnected on the internet.

Friendship renewed, today we enjoy a healthy and supportive exchange of monthly news and mutual encouragement.

Paul lives today in Chicago with Jeff, his partner of 20-plus years. I enter my senior years in Hawaiʻi, single and unattached. The irony is not appreciated on my end.

Somewhere About Mile Marker 85

A couple of miles past the last turnoff toward Miloliʻi, in a field on a farm in south Big Island, there is a zebra. I mean, really? A zebra? In South Kona?

Over a period of ten years, Ocean View on the southern flanks of the Big Island was my on-and-off home. Town shopping in Kona, on the drive home, I passed this odd site. Some farmer on the *makai* (ocean) side of the highway raised exotic animals. Among long-horned African cattle, donkeys, and some strange sheep and elk, the strangest sight is that zebra.

Invariably, there are a couple of cars pulled off the roadside with tourists snapping shots on iPhones. Out of place, a misfit, the odd one—the zebra in South Kona always unsettles me.

I identify with that zebra. I often feel that I'm the one oddity that doesn't quite belong. Not just the "belonging in Hawaiʻi"—it's larger than that, and deeper too. A universal, human condition—don't we all search our entire lives to find some communion with larger humanity?

My feeling different had its roots in my childhood. My father never really wanted a first son—he secretly desired a male lover. Our relationship was forever complicated by this unmentionable dynamic. As a result, I grew up feeling like I could not measure up, like I never quite belonged, like I was forever different and apart. In addition to that inner turmoil, our family moved every couple of years. I never had a best friend until Elsie Prahm and I bonded when I was in junior high school. But even that was an oddity—she was sixty-five and I was fourteen.

I always fit awkwardly or not at all:

- I couldn't get the Easter eggs in the park at age 2½.
- I had buck teeth and needed braces at age twelve.
- Late in puberty, I hated taking a shower after gym class with the other boys.
- The 4.0 nerd in high school, I didn't play sports like the other guys.
- Gay—out and proud at age twenty-six, but certainly not one of the norm.
- Self-identified as "an adult child of an alcoholic."
- The haole boy living in Hawai'i.
- The monk—spiritual but not religious; contemplative but ill-suited for monastery; identified as Episcopalian yet agnostic to the core.
- The one, lone man in every quilting group.

Can everyone jot off a list of such oddity and not belonging? Probably, yes. But does sharing oddity with others make me any less "the odd one out?"

CHAPTER ELEVEN

MY NIGHT MOONBOW

Living in the Forest

Like elven folk—but we don't have elves in Hawai'i. Or like menehune—Hawai'i's legendary race of small people. We were forest dwellers—tree people.

A favorite home was the customized owner-builder house that Henry Kim and I shared on 3rd Avenue in Mauna Loa Estates on an unpopulated, dead-end street on the edge of Volcano Village. Her beautifully golden natural wood with forest green trim blended with the woods. A second-story open-air lanai with clear vinyl roof panels defied distinction between indoors and outdoors. Graceful tendrils of *hāpu'u* fern reached over the railings, offering us to join fingers—testimony that we belonged as members of the forest family. Succulent spikes of red *lehua* blossoms of 'ōhi'a trees attracted 'apapane (indigenous honeycreeper) and Japanese white-eye (introduced). No need CD player—we enjoyed morning Haydn concertos, sung by birds in our treetops.

Mornings were bright and cheery, so pleasant as the sun burned away the night chill. Clouding over before noon, by mid-afternoon, we were living in the cloud bank. The foggy mist *(ka noe)* crept across the drive—a bit haunting—a clue to the approaching chill of evening.

From the day it was completed, that lānai was where we lived. The rest of the house relegated to cooking, bathing, and storage, we ate, relaxed, read, talked, slept, and had sex on that lānai. Our abode was the forest.

On my first Hawai'i vacation, I had been so attracted by the whole notion of living in spaces where you couldn't tell whether you were indoors or outdoors. Our Volcano home replicated that. The rain forest fed our souls.

Cracks in the Earth

Orange-red glow, visible only after dark. Madame Pele spitting her fiery vomit, spewing it through a tunnel of her own creation. Lava tubes—Pele's expressway from mountain to the sea. Invited guests, we were promised front-row seats to the nightly performance, some thirteen years running.

Summer 1996. My partner, Henry; his mom, Peggy; his sister Nancy; and I were enjoying a long weekend in our Volcano home. On Saturday, we ventured on a nighttime outing down Chain of Craters Road. Arriving before dark on the southern edge of the flow, we ventured some fifty yards out onto the lava. Seated and ready for the evening show, we knew that night viewing could be unpredictable. The lead actress, Pele, was reputed to be fickle. Distant flow that night, lava entry into the ocean more than a mile off, a disappointing performance to a returning audience.

No matter. We chattered, enjoyed the warm night breeze, the hint of sea spray, the full moon rising. There was enough moonlight so Peggy could walk sure-footed across the irregular braided lava back to the road.

Piling into our Range Rover, we headed up the mountain toward home. Rounding a curve, my eyes caught a shimmer in the night sky. Pulling off the road at the top of Hilina Pali, I prompted everyone to climb out, where we gazed up into the night sky in astonished amazement.

We stared speechless at a night rainbow arching in the distance from *pali* (cliff) to the ocean. Spanning the color spectrum, hues skewed toward violet or black. Casting an eerie spectacle, a perfectly arched moonbow. Everything in that moment was charged with bewildering mana. The night air was electrified. We were mesmerized by this heavenly manifestation before our unbelieving eyes.

For time immeasurable, the four of us stood, entranced and silent, fixated on a vision of inexplicable power. Few words spoken—no need for language. Intuitively we grasped that we were chosen to receive a rare gift. Unaware of its import or meaning, we were passive recipients. We stood in solemnity, gazing up in reverence at that which was offered us.

Not One Word Spoken

After the night rainbow—silence. Seventeen miles from Hilina Pali to Volcano, not a peep. Wheels pummeled against blacktop—nothing more. At home, whispered voices, fearful of disrupting the mystical night's enchantment.

What had happened? What was its meaning? Peggy had heard of night rainbows but never expected to see one. Henry and Nancy were stunned and silent. Just audible, I uttered, "I have a book, *Tales from the Night Rainbow,* by Koko Willis."

Determined to learn more, I researched and found one quote, "Thus seeing a rainbow at night can be interpreted as divine interventions that offer you a glimmer of hope at the time of trouble."

Our night moonbow had more insight than Henry and I. In 1996, we were charmed by a different lover. With his seductive allure, Sweet Success had us worshipping at his altar. Our vows proclaimed, we waited for him to declare fealty. The darlings of the local Hawaiian clothing industry, we bathed in lavish praise and accolades. Sweet Success had made us drunkards with his addictive potions.

We took no notice of his early infidelities. Kmart, Walmart, Ross Dress for Less, Marshall's—ready-to-wear for a pittance. Cartier, Chanel, Gucci, Fendi—finer allure for the wealthy. Our night moonbow had come and gone—she offered no false pretense. Sweet Success lingered, pledging false allegiance to disguise his betrayal. We took no notice until too late.

Our small Island business faltered, then slipped into decline, eventually into bankruptcy. The years following challenged my spirit and my calling to belong in Hawai'i more than any other in my life.

Sweet Success (the worldly kind) can be elusive and fleeting. His spell undeserving of commitment to marriage.

The night rainbow experience is long past. One brief encounter some twenty-five years ago. Yet I can see her as vividly this evening as I did that night on Hilina Pali along Chain of Craters Road. Each time I recall her, I shudder, then shift. Quiet the chatter in my brain. Sit still, present in the calm assurance of my night moonbow.

Challenges and troubles, they are passing. They begin. They have their time. But they always end. Often I emerge with some newly gained insight, some new direction and focus. I can always rely on the memory of my night moonbow to gird me with strength and endurance. She is forever my gift of divine intervention.

Grandpa Glasener's White Hair

Not a tinge of blue or blond or gray or white—snow white. I expected to inherit Grandpa's white hair.

The trait I remember most about Grandpa was his stoicism. He was a rock—constant, steady, determined. A man of few words—when he spoke, I listened. Grandpa's stoicism—I knew I could never inherit that. I admired it; I would never possess it. Mr. Up-Down-All-Over-the-Emotional-Map? But the white hair—I pinned my hopes on that.

My mom had ash blond hair. She called it "mousy blond." When Mom turned sixty, her hair turned Grandpa's snow white. For thirty years, I adored my mom's white hair. I knew I was next to inherit it.

Mom was a woman of faith. Through every storm and trial and tribulation, she remained constant. Faith in God—that was pivotal. But Mom's faith extended to everything and everyone. She believed in her family, her church, her community, her world. Mom held steady, knowing that love would always triumph. Mom's faith—I knew I had not inherited that. I was always asking, "Why?" Like my father, I doubted more often than trusted. But the white hair—my hopes rested on that.

I have Mom's mousy, ash blond hair. When I turned sixty, a few promising strands lightened on my temples. Over the next decade—nothing. I'm seventy-one now. I have ash blond hair with a few strands of gray. At least I have it. I didn't lose it like brother Jeff. But I did not inherit what is rightfully mine.

I won't have white hair. I cannot be stoic. I am not a man of unquestioning faith. Blond hair, mood swings, always questioning—that's my inheritance.

Your Mother-in-Law

When that woman keeps an ugly blue plastic container, the one with a sponge and soapy water with a tinge of bleach, sitting right beside the sink, DO NOT remove it. Not even for a festive family holiday.

Thanksgiving Day in our Volcano home was Henry's and my favorite day of the year, and 1996 was the best. All three Kim sisters plus four generations of extended family joined us with Momma Peggy. We were a hearty clan, preparing to gather around the table.

The fireplace was blazing, keeping the early winter chill at bay. Oven heat added to our comfort, warming our spirits and delighting our senses with all the aromas of a family Thanksgiving meal. Everything typical—a platter of turkey, apple-sausage–water chestnut stuffing, mashed potatoes, sticky rice (a must-have in any local family feast), candied yams, all-over-everything gravy. Oh, you know—the usuals. Which included my odd Stark family tradition— scalloped oysters.

But tensions lingered in the air, even as we circled the table to share the meal. The previous evening a disagreement had sparked between Henry's mom and his lover (me). Peggy lived with us and faithfully cared for our Volcano home while we were busy in Honolulu with business. She kept an ugly plastic container of soapy bleach water right on the counter beside the sink. Deeming the thing unsightly, I had emptied it and retired the container to the cupboard.

Incensed, Peggy had not spoken to me since the evening prior. While everyone hustled around preparing dishes, Peggy sat and pouted, refusing to give a hand to help. What could I do? I forged ahead. We had twelve hungry mouths to feed.

The family circle completed, we joined hands. Silence settled. I prayed.

"Dear heavenly God, the Source and Keeper of us all, we gather on this day of Thanksgiving. We have so much. We enjoy such beauty, such bounty in this forest home. Family gathered together in joy and fun and gratitude. We thank You for this time together, for this meal, for all the hands who have made it happen. And especially today, God, we thank you for Momma. Her hands, her feet, her labor keep this home safe and welcome. We thank you for this gift of time spent together with Momma in our home. Be with her, be with us today and every day. And now, let's eat! 'Āmene."

Peggy in tears, rounding the table, gave me a long hearty hug. We all dove in and feasted together.

CHAPTER TWELVE

BFF—DON'T LEAVE HOME WITHOUT ONE

Nikki Picked Up the Eraser

"Yeees, may I help you?"

I had just tossed it across the room divider into the row of desks where she sat, working on her charting. It was the tool we devised to get one another's attention since our desks sat out of sightline from one another.

Nikki Bracken was my go-to at Care Resource Hawai'i, whenever I needed a nurse to assess a problem with a client. When Nikki wanted a physical therapist, I got the call.

Charting was due every other Monday for payroll processing. On Sunday evenings, Nikki and I were workmates, cramming to finish our last-minute home health documentation.

"It's nine thirty. I have ten more notes, and I've run out of gas."

"I have fifteen notes to go. You win," she retorted.

I tempted her. "Leftover birthday cake in the conference room."

"Ahh! Sugar high to finish the evening! Let's go."

Friendships are always born around food.

It's All About the Wedding Dress

Spring 1999, Lua Poe became topic number one with Nikki Bracken. Having obtained a visa, Lua was moving to Oʻahu to live with Nikki. With a couple of weeks' notice, all Nikki's friends pummeled her with questions. We knew of Lua, her romantic partner during her decade-long life in American Sāmoa. Now we needed details...

...which were answered in the form of a stocky, laughter-filled man with one glass eye.

Just like that, he was here. Nikki's Makiki apartment had made one impression upon me. It was so definitively a woman's space. Now it was home to a reunited couple.

My partner Henry and I met Lua a couple of days after his arrival, sharing dinner at Silver Dragon Restaurant in Kapālama. Not one for lengthy conversation, Lua was friendly and jovial. We laughed our way through hot tea, beef with tomato, lemon chicken, pork with snowshoe peas, and sticky rice. I forget the cookie fortunes, but they were bright. Verdict in—Lua was welcome. *E komo mai. Talofa.*

In May 2000, Nikki and Lua were getting married. Henry and I offered a wedding present— Henry would design Nikki's wedding dress. Unable to arrange a personal fitting, Henry worked from measurements and tailored a lightweight, white shift with an overlaying sheer fabric.

When Nikki received the dress the week of the wedding, it was one and a half times too big. Not a pro at working with plus sizes, Henry had missed. A loyal friend helped Nikki take the dress in. On wedding day, she glowed in her one-of-a-kind, slightly altered, designer wedding dress.

Losing a Dear Friend

Not a thing to which I am accustomed. Even though I am now seventy-one, I'm not ready to make it one.

In spring 2018, Nikki was in a bad way. Hospitalized three times with atrial fibrillation between February and April, Nikki suffered severe shortness of breath which made it a challenge just to walk to the bathroom. Having moved in 2005 to Union City, California, to be connected with her grandchildren, Nikki remained my dear friend—now at long distance.

I booked a flight to Oakland for a five-day visit. Touted as an overdue reunion, privately, I was prepared to bid my friend aloha for her predictable departure into the great unknown.

In early May, befuddled by her lack of improvement, Nikki changed cardiologists. The new doc diagnosed congestive heart failure. Medications changed and improvement followed. When I landed in Oakland on May 31, Nikki greeted me with open arms and working lungs.

"Hooray! Let's have fun!" Nikki and I concurred.

Nikki Bracken-Poe with Ric at the Ferry Building, San Francisco

Saturday, Union City Farmers' Market. I went nuts! Scads of fresh produce, the kind I never get in Hawai'i. I loaded my bags with fresh apricots, oysters in the shell, fresh greens, sweet corn, and some fresh herbs. Good eatin' ahead!

There was one disappointment—my aim of that venture had been rhubarb. It was spring and I wanted to make fresh rhubarb pie, my all-time favorite. No rhubarb at the market. Some vendors asked, "What's that?"

Over the years, I have determined one "must-do" in any trip to the Bay area—the Ferry Building. An architectural delight, completed in 1898 by A. Page Brown in the Beaux-Arts style, the Ferry Building was restored from decline in 2000. The 660-foot-long Great Nave is now home to a splendid bustling open market. I never do San Francisco without the Ferry Building.

Monday morning, we boarded a passenger boat from Union City across the bay, docking at our destination. My shopping spree lived up to expectations. At my first and favorite destination, Cowgirl Creamery, I savored the doting expertise of a concessionaire who guided us through a half dozen samples of cheeses with indescribable complexities in flavor. I chose three. Stalking up and down the great corridor, I added goodies to my bag—three kinds of fresh mushrooms; fresh-baked, aromatic breads; chocolates; a $38 bottle of wine. Having depleted my allotted cash allowance, Nikki and I split a deli-fresh turkey sandwich with a black raspberry bottled water.

Not hungry, Lua wandered, while we two pals sat in the sunshine and watched seagulls swoop about the pier.

Tuesday morning demanded one last trip away from home. Fresh rhubarb having evaded all inquiries, I settled for two packages of frozen from Whole Foods.

Time for the chef to spring into action. Pies! The main course would be a beef pie. Meat simmered to exquisite tenderness in market herbs, then baked in a casserole with gourmet mushrooms and veggies. My favorite crust, a sinful combination of butter and lard with just enough flour to hold it together.

Nikki's daughter, Penny, and her family first declined an invitation, then showed up near mealtime. "Heyyyy! Come on in and enjoy the feast!" Fresh apricots and cheeses with wine for *pūpū* (appetizers). Everyone scooped out moderate portions of pot pie, then requested seconds. And, of course, fresh rhubarb pie for dessert—the pie plate was emptied.

For years, I had complained to Nikki, "Kids today! Your grandchildren have no social skills. Parents don't expect their children to display proper manners when interacting with adults." Well! I was privileged to spend a whole half hour on the lānai with Nola and Harper with our pie plates in hand. The kids were in hysterics that Uncle Ric did not know what a meme was. They tried to explain—largely in vain. I still don't get the concept. But I did get to forge priceless memories with the kids, which I savor in ways they can never comprehend.

BFF—don't ever leave home without one.

An Iconic Family Photo

Grandpa Glasener, sitting on a log, holding my toddler brother Jeff on his lap. I am sitting beside Grandpa, one hand on Grandpa's knee. Four years old—hair neatly combed, smiling, dressed up in shorts, boy's shirt, and saddle shoes, I can see a bit of angst in my smile. Probably because balancing on the log with my feet dangling, I need that one hand on Grandpa's knee for reassurance.

In the photo, that log is lying in the yard outside Grandpa's cabin at Bark Point on the southern shore of Lake Superior. Once a tall fir tree perched too close to the cliff above the lakeshore, steady erosion of the bank had made the tree unstable. Chopped down, the reclining log regained its fortitude as a perfect place for a family snapshot. That cabin, that shoreline is arguably my favorite place in the world.

What is it about that photo that makes it iconic in my memory? The log, the lake in the background, the north woods, the cabin just out of view, the sunshine reflecting on our faces—all of those portray a world of bright promises.

But it's my hand on Grandpa's knee—that's the key. Grandpa was my rock, my anchor. I idolized him. I knew I could trust Grandpa to never let me fall off that log.

Chapter Thirteen
KAʻU KUMU KUIKI—MY QUILTING TEACHER

I Can't Teach a Man with Big Hands Like Yours

Aunty Vi swipes away my request that she teach me Hawaiian quilting. I don't protest. Knowing Violet Hue, I know that no one wins an argument with Aunty Vi.

A week later, I repeat my request. "Aunty, please, teach me! I heard your sister Peggy call out to me just like she was still in the room, 'Ric, you need to learn Hawaiian quilting.'"

"Ahhh, you're just one know-it-all haole. I can't teach you." It stings but only delays my determination.

Again, I wait a few days. "Aunty, please. I promise. I will listen and do as you say."

"Oh, I guess we can try. We'll see if you can do my tiny stitches." Three times I asked, just like the old Hawaiian way. An omen?

On a bright, sunny Sunday in July 1998, Henry and I take Aunty Vi to brunch at Nani Loa Hotel.

After a satisfying buffet, Aunty and I sit across from one another at a table on the lawn beside Hilo Bay.

"Let me see what you've done so far." She picks up my *mokihana* pillow project, depicting the fragrant berry of the mokihana tree of the island of Kaua'i, the one I started four years earlier and never could finish. She holds a needle and demonstrates the needle-turn applique.

"You make it look so easy, Aunty! I'll never…" Doubting Ric.

"You just do it. Don't worry about your stitches. The first two are just for practice. After the third one, I will look at your stitches," she reassures and redirects me. "And one other thing. Always pull your thread straight toward your heart. Every time. That way you sew love into every stitch."

Aunty Vi's words were so simple. I will never comprehend how she reached inside my soul that Sunday afternoon and changed the direction and focus of my life. But she did. And forever after, I measure that day—before Aunty, after Aunty. Before Hawaiian quilting, after Hawaiian quilting.

The Woman Who Taught Me to Quilt

This is Aunty Vi's story, small kind.

Violet Grace Suzuki was born in Kalapana in April 1928. With the frenzy of anti-Japanese sentiment in World War II, the boys changed the family name to their grandfather's, Wilson. One step further back brings us to the Hawaiian name of Violet's grandmother, Kaliko Ka'aukai.

Family history stories were woven abundantly into gatherings and conversations. Wondering whether these were exaggerated family tales, I listened with a healthy skepticism but never challenged what I heard. I sensed that the Kaʻaukai family was of some significant, kahuna background. One story of Uncle Masa's claimed that the twins depicted flanking the Kamehameha royal crest were direct ancestors. Aunty once alluded to family origins on Molokaʻi. In another story, she told of the family name being associated with the island chant, "Keawe o Hawaiʻi."

Lacking any validation of these tales, I recall a couple of valid accounts. My partner Henry recalled an early childhood event with his great-grandmother—a towering, forceful presence in Henry's memory. When the family entered Kawaihaʻo Church one Sunday, walking behind Kaliko, everyone in the congregation rose to their feet and bowed in obeisance as the family matriarch marched down the center aisle to a front pew.

Another tale was told by Aunty Vi. Each year at Merrie Monarch time, Aunty and her friend Margaret gathered flowers and greens in the forest above Kaumana on Saddle Road and made an assortment of *lei poʻo* (head lei). Aunty took her wares to sell outside Edith Kanakaʻole Stadium on the weekend of hula competition. Arriving late, Aunty announced herself by her family name, Kaʻaukai. The other vendors shuffled to make space for Aunty at the front booth. It was a show of respect for a *kupuna* of an honored Hawaiian family.

This was the woman who took my heart and turned it inside out, changing my life forever. Aunty Vi taught me to pray with needle and thread.

I Did Not Have a BFF Until I Was Fourteen

Elsie Prahm was sixty-five. Our story was *Harold and Maude*, minus the sexual overtones.

As part of my summer lawn service in Rowley, Iowa, I was hired to mow the lawn for the widow. In time, other farm chores were added. Over a couple of years, I gained the unofficial title of farmhand. Elsie and I enjoyed a friendship, vital to both of us for the remainder of her life.

On long weekends during college, I took a Greyhound bus south from St. Paul to Independence, Iowa, where I spent the weekend with Elsie. While we would invariably venture on some country outing, most of our weekend passed on the living room sofa. Elsie and I could talk for hours on end, sharing stories, politics, religion, my college life, her small-town gossip. There was never much quiet time between us.

On one of my visits, I became acutely aware of one difference. While we sat whittling away the hours chatting, Elsie was productively crocheting a scarf, while I sat with idle hands.

"Elsie, will you teach me how to crochet?" I asked.

"Of course, I would love to help you learn," she replied. "I knew a country doctor who enjoyed a nightly habit of knitting." I guess it seemed important to her to establish the legitimacy of a man working with needle and thread.

By the time I boarded the bus back to school, I had a crochet hook, a pattern book, and wool yarn in brown, orange, and bright gold. God-awful color combinations at that!

Completing that first project over the coming months, it's a marvel that I continued. My finished afghan was an awkward construction, measuring a full foot wider at the top than at its base. My stitching had loosened and matured that much as I worked the long rows. But, man, was it warm! I wrapped that afghan around me for countless winter nights in Minnesota.

My first afghan also marked a characteristic that endures. Never beginning with a small easy project, always I want to jump right to the grand challenging design. From the very beginning, I was striving to become a Hawaiian quilt master.

CHAPTER FOURTEEN

ALL PAU

"What a Fucking Bitch!"
(Ted Yoho, Hooting at AOC)

The following day, March 28, 2020, Alexandria Ocasio-Cortez spoke on the House floor on behalf of the worth and dignity of all women.

Sitting on my sofa, tears welled up in my eyes. "How could any man, especially one serving…?"

. . .

Spring 1975—Ginny and I, newly married the previous August, had rented a first apartment in Summit Hills, a quiet affluent neighborhood in St. Paul, Minnesota. Married life had begun with a joyous swirl of energy. Ginny loved her work as an RN at St. Luke's Hospital. I had begun my junior year in the Physical Therapy Program at the University of Minnesota.

But the road to our happy future had darkened. It would be another two years before I could surrender and acknowledge that I was a gay man. In 1975, I was wrestling my demons—alone, secretively, with no one knowing.

On one evening, Ginny and I were arguing as we stood in the doorway between bedroom and hallway. Sparring with words, our tensions heightened. My coiled repressed anger swelled, then snapped.

"Damn it! Back off me! You're such a bitch!"

Ginny flinched and pulled away, admonishing me with a voice to equal my own, "Don't you EVER call me that again!"

I could see in that moment I had struck deeply, wounding something in Ginny. Ashamed of my behavior, I turned and slithered away. I was frantic to escape and deny the harm I had done. After all, I was a women's liberation guy. I respected women equally and with the utmost honor.

But I ran away. And I never ever spoke of that incident again.

.   .   .

Alexandria Ocasio-Cortez shot an arrow, pierced my denial, and exposed the abscess inside. It took me most of one week to unmask the connection between Ted Yoho and Ric Stark. It took another five months to speak words of apology and amends.

My brain cycled countless rationalizations to keep silent. "It was forty-four years ago. Let it be. Ginny healed long ago. A new marriage, two girls, a successful career, grandchildren. Don't drag up old bygones that are long forgotten. Leave it buried."

But it is not buried, is it? There is no single moment in my life that holds more regret and shame. And somewhere inside I know that Ginny has not forgotten. I know that I never apologized or said the words that must be said.

Ginny, I am sorry. No woman deserves to hear that word hurled at her, especially not from the man who had sworn an oath to be her protector and companion in life. Ginny, I'm sorry. You deserved better. You deserve better.

. . .

Thirty minutes after finishing the essay above, I emailed it to Ginny. Twenty-four hours later, she replied.

> The episode is not a scar. Actually, it was a stimulus to stand up for myself and set limits. It set me on an assertive path. I am pleased to see successful women role modeling that behavior for young women now. The incident started me on a course that I am certain had a positive impact in my professional career as well as my personal life. While pleasing other people (as I had been taught to do growing up) was still important, I would no longer compromise my own integrity to do so.

I wrote back.

> Ginny, I am so pleased and reassured to know how you transformed hurt into strength. Something

about our shared Leo energies that helps us use fire for building and growth? And thank you. Thank you for sharing that with me. Now I can walk forward and live in peace, comforted and reassured that the wound I caused harmed only me—seeding in you a drive and growth toward fortitude.

Forgiveness—a most potent gift. Receiving it from another—priceless. Allowing it of oneself is life nurturing. Yes, even forty-four years too late.

Outside the Door, the Short, Chewed End of Aka's Leash

But no Aka.

December 18, 2000. My Chow Chow and I had walked together along the isolated roads of Mauna Loa Estates to visit neighbors Ricia and Nick. They had internet connection; Henry and I didn't. Needing to do online research, I got carried away. Several hours had lapsed when I realized, "It's getting late."

I bid my farewells and mahalo to Nick and Ricia. Outside the door, I found the short, chewed end of Aka's leash. But no Aka.

A panicked jog six blocks home. Arriving breathless, I threw the door open and bounded up the stairs, right into the fury and fire of Henry.

"WHERE HAVE YOU BEEN! WHAT WERE YOU THINKING? DON'T YOU CARE FOR YOUR PRECIOUS DOG? WHAT'S WRONG WITH YOU!" Henry was livid. Missing my presence,

Aka had chewed through her leash and run home alone. She was fine. Henry was not.

An argument ensued. Argument? Outrage—yelling—screaming—storming through the house, hounded by rage. I cannot stand conflict. I will do quite a bit to evade it. Running down the stairs into the ground-floor room, I sought escape. Henry did not relent. Pursuing me, he charged, screaming at the back of my neck.

Out of nowhere, a fist plows into my face. My glasses fly, landing on the far side of the room. Stunned, I am paralyzed. I don't know physical violence. It's never been done by me—it's never happened to me.

I shake myself from my stupor, retrieve my glasses, bound up the stairs to evade Henry and the violence. He pursues, refusing to back off. Up and down the stairs, tearing through the house. I yank open the freezer door to grab the jar with the last $1,100 of my cashed-out retirement savings.

Henry's words threaten me, "If you touch that money, you won't leave this house alive! Go! We don't want you here anyway. You're just one more damn haole and you don't belong here, and you know it!"

I recoil and head for the stairs a third time. Henry is hot on my heels—still pursuing, still challenging. I turn, desperate to stop his assault. I shove at his chest. He loses his balance, falling backwards and landing on the steps.

I clamber down the stairs. "Aka, come!" Dutifully, she obeys. Together we rush off into the Volcano night.

Twelve years of a business, a partnership, a Volcano/Honolulu life—ended. In one instant, it was all *pau*.

CHAPTER FIFTEEN

QUILTING BUDDIES

Ad on Craigslist

Need woman to teach beginning Hawaiian quilting. Calling the number provided, I spoke with Donna Masaniai. "While I am neither a woman nor Hawaiian, I do love to teach Hawaiian quilting." Donna, owner of a small quilt shop in Pāhala, and I agreed on a teaching stint and began an endearing and enduring friendship.

Over the next five years, Donna and I shared frequent quilting fun. Donna's husband Tui was living and working toward retirement in Washington state. Making trips several times each year to visit her husband, Donna would ask me to mind the shop. I would live in her house and take care of her fourteen-year-old dog, Maile, and attend to the trickle of shop customers. Everything about our life circumstances worked compatibly and we deepened our friendship.

One memorable episode with Donna occurred in 2013. I decided to dye my own cotton fabrics for my quilts. Living off-grid and hauling my water, I needed a place with ample water for the rinse. Donna volunteered—she didn't yet realize what saying "Yes" to Ric might entail. One afternoon in the middle of my hand-dyeing project, I had more than a dozen three-yard fabrics in an array of bold colors—cerulean blues, jade greens, bright oranges, sunshine yellows, fuchsia pinks—spread out across her lawn, drying in the sunshine. Needing a break, Donna and I retired to the front lānai for some cool breeze and refreshment. Scanning the kaleidoscope of color, spread across the green grass, we cracked up and enjoyed our iced teas.

Located a couple of miles off Māmalahoa Belt Highway and some eleven miles above South Point, Discovery Harbour is a community association plopped right in the middle of the country. My anchor quilt *hui* (club), Ka Lae Quilters, met every Thursday in the community center.

Introduced to the group by Donna, I was the lone man in the group. My reputation as a Hawaiian quilter having preceded me, I was introduced to newcomers as "our Hawaiian quilt master." During winter months, we often crowded some thirty women around the dozen work tables. Jokingly called the rooster in the hen house—with thirty women cackling at once—the description didn't fall far from the truth.

At Ka Lae, we didn't fuss with formality or structure. A welcoming, friendly group of neighbors, we simply gathered every week for fun and communion—and, of course, shared quilting projects. Good people and good times are universally enjoyed among quilters. The camaraderie at Ka Lae

Quilters holds that special place. It's home. Such are the memories that weave the fabrics of friendships among quilting buddies.

Still Home

Ka Lae Quilters is still home, even three years after I left Big Island. Without officers or dues, these neighbors have gathered weekly for over thirty years. Friendships are deep and authentic. The fellowship in Ka Lae is what quilters everywhere aspire to achieve.

Much of that community flavor comes from the core old-timers. Diane Farrar might unofficially be called the club secretary. Keeper of addresses and emails, Diane sends out notices of upcoming meetings, as well as announcements of members' changes or challenges or illnesses. Diane works faithfully to keep the group connected and in tune with recent news.

My favorite time spent with Diane was a Wednesday evening in 2013, shared in Hilo at the Merrie Monarch Hula Festival. Open to the public with performances by non-competing *hula hālau* (dance schools), Wednesday night is the preview for this world-famous hula competition. 2013 was special—Merrie Monarch's fiftieth anniversary celebration.

Four of us from Ka Lae Quilters had tickets and shared seats near the stage. Diane and I sat and chattered and reminisced as we watched a parade of performances celebrating the history of Merrie Monarch. Marveling to see Tracie Lopez and Maelia

Lobenstein usher their own hālau on stage to perform, I had watched both of these women when they performed and won the honored title of Miss Aloha Hula twenty-five years earlier.

The evening culminated for Diane, Suzanne, Teri, and me when we watched Robert Cazimero bring his hālau on stage to perform. Dancer Kilohana Domingo, crippled by complications of disease and barely able to walk, was assisted by his hula brothers and supported as he walked onto the stage. Sitting in a chair while the others stood, Kilohana danced riveting hula with his companions from thirty years earlier. Diane, Suzanne, and I wept. Kilohana had been the women's *kumu 'ōlelo* (Hawaiian language teacher). I was crying because a gay man had such courage. Diane and Suzanne were crying for more personal reasons.

As I recall the memory, Cazimero's hālau is so much like Ka Lae Quilters—friends who will do whatever it takes to share and to support one another in our art, in our lives.

It Seems Odd to Me

I have such dedication for an art form that involves sewing. Although I have never been tested, I know that I have some form of dyslexia involving spatial orientation.

Vivid in my memory is my first day of kindergarten in Hudson, Iowa. After school, I bounded off the school bus, eager to show Mommy what I had done. Taking me into the hallway and holding up my paper in the mirror, Mom showed me my name, "R-i-c-k-y". Then she turned the paper toward me. At once I recognized and saw what I had written on the paper, "y-k-c-i-R".

Somehow, bright and quick enough to adapt and rearrange my brain, I don't remember suffering any of the prolonged torments that many dyslexic children endure. But I have never been a fast reader. After failed attempts at speed reading, I plug along at 150 words a minute. I can hear myself when I read, pronouncing each word silently in my head. I am stupefied by the notion of skimming or speed reading.

When I sew on a sewing machine, I predictably sew pieces together backward some ninety percent of the time. I study the pattern. Check it twice to make certain I am getting it right. "Okay, now sew them together." Hold it up. There you have it— backward again!

Thankfully, my appointed art form of Hawaiian quilting is nearly one hundred percent hand stitching. I marvel at piecers, who assemble and create such intricate works of geometry. I could never do it. When I do need to work at my sewing machine, I have two tools at hand—a pair of scissors and my seam ripper—essential items for a man who confuses left with right!

Chapter Sixteen

PONO

Un-Retiring at Sixty-Eight with the Best Boss Ever

Sixty-eight is not thirty-eight, just as seventy is not the new forty.

Rusty like a door hinge left in the rain, my technical skills were lagging, and my computer proficiency was horrid. Johhna Johnson, Director of Bayada Home Health Care, sat patiently one desk away from me during my entire first month of orientation, June 2018. No matter how small or how often my questions, Johhna patiently helped me through the learning curve.

The ninth director of a home health agency that I've worked under in Hawai'i, Johhna Johnson is the best. Much credit belongs with Bayada, our agency. Who would expect that a private, for-profit, mainland company would be the one to rise above the others in cooperation and team building? Johhna embodies and employs the company philosophy: *Compassion. Excellence. Reliability.*

At the end of my three-month employment, I suffered a meltdown. Twenty years earlier I had managed a full-time caseload with proficiency. Now I simply could not cope. After two weeks of mental-health time off, I submitted my resignation. Johhna accepted with empathy. One week later she offered me a different path.

"Ric, why don't you come back to work on a per-diem basis? You tell me what you can handle, and we'll make it work. I know you have the skills and I really want you to succeed."

Three years later I work three half-days a week, just the right caseload to pay the bills and give me a few $$$ for my savings account. No other supervisor ever managed that kind of empathetic oversight and support. Johhna gets my vote every time.

Best memory—one year ago, Bayada needed some extra help in the Hilo office. Reluctantly, Johhna agreed to loan me out for four days a week. On that temporary one-month term, I loved working out of the Hilo office. Smaller, more family-style, the staff was well-suited to my informal work manner. When it was time to terminate my off-island loan, I requested a meeting with Johhna.

She began our meeting, "I hope you're not going to tell me you're moving back to Hilo. I told them they could 'borrow' you. I don't want to hurt anybody to keep you. But if I need to, I will!"

I laughed and replied, "Now there's the Johhna behind the calm exterior. I always knew you were a lot tougher than you let on. No, I just want to discuss my hours."

Thanks, Johhna. You da bes'.

Anomalies Keep Happening

I venture into Hawai'i nature and find myself transported into a dimension that simply is other than planet Earth.

In December 2004, I was invited by a co-worker, Barb, to join her friend Jane and husband Dave on a Mauna Kea expedition. Dave worked in one of the telescopes—Canada-France, I think. We were to join a tour of the telescope from the inside!

At 8:00 a.m. on December 25, we arrived at the summit—a bright, crispy Christmas morning. An amazing tour, the Mauna Kea summit is spectacular on any day. The telescope towered over several floors. Walking through several hallways on different levels, we emerged with a new view of the gigantic telescope. Awe-inspiring, the mammoth lens was covered during the day. I could sense the power and wonder of peering into our distant universe.

It was late morning when we left the summit. A few hundred yards below Mauna Kea's summit, a jeep trail veered off to one side. Before it began, the road ended. We parked and walked a footpath over a small rise...

...and into a different world. Descending on the far side of the mound, we approached the edge of a small body of water, Lake Waiau. I had heard of it. I knew that Lake Waiau holds essential spiritual significance for Hawaiians. I was inadequately prepared for the experience, for what was about to occur.

Physically, Lake Waiau is similar to the many high mountain lakes that I often encountered while hiking the mountain peaks in Colorado in my younger days. Nestled in a sheltered, rocky dish, this small body of water rested quietly before us. I mumbled under my breath, "How can a lake be up on top of this barren mountain?" The other-world reality is difficult to remember. The lake was perhaps 150 feet across— I'm not really certain.

From the moment my feet touched the shoreline, I was gone, transported into a dimension unknown to me. My eyes, ears, nose, skin were all sensing the physical reality of Lake Waiau atop Mauna Kea on the Big Island of Hawai'i in the middle of the Pacific Ocean on planet Earth. But my soul and my spirit were transported somewhere different. I felt wetness running down my cheeks. Stunned, I stood immobile. This tiny lake was the world's *piko*, its navel and umbilical cord, right where my feet were touching. I could feel the Christmas miracle. Birthing the world, this physical reality, this very existence—all of it emanating forth from this Lake Waiau.

Unable to step, my body was not responding to earthly cues. Barb and Jane moved, coursing the lake's shoreline. In some time, Jane, a hula dancer, paused directly opposite me. Standing across the lake, she began to chant.

My feet sprang to respond. I began to dance a rhythmic hula, one I had learned from my friend

Susan Floyd. There we celebrated the Christmas miracle of birth. Jane, the hula dancer, chanted. I, the Hawaiian language student, danced.

If you ever hear anyone mention Lake Waiau, stop and listen. You may be invited to the very piko of creation.

It's Not Difficult to Hide a Secret

May 1976. While the nation prepared for the bicentennial celebration, I was one of thirty-two students who had finished finals in the physical therapy program at the University of Minnesota in Minneapolis. In the three-week hiatus between finals and graduation, fourteen of us stuffed backpacks and bodies into cars and headed north to Ely, Minnesota, entry to the US-Canadian Boundary Waters. Celebrating together, we would spend ten days canoeing, portaging, and camping in the north woods.

Approaching my twenty-seventh birthday, I had trekked a different kind of journey during the months prior. A pivotal realization in my life, I had accepted that I was a gay man. Holding this epiphany private, it would be two months before I ripped open my closet door and came out to the woman I had married, to family and friends, to the world.

Some twenty years of struggle, turmoil, and inner torment had ended. At age twenty-six, I could finally accept who I was and be happy and at peace with my true self.

It is challenging to share gay coming out with a wider circle of fellow beings. Almost all persecuted peoples struggle against prejudice, which is visible and apparent to all. There is something uniquely tormenting about being one of a hidden, hated minority. Jews trying to hide in 1930s Germany, fair-skin blacks trying to pass as white—these people may identify with unmasking a hidden self. Most of us gay men and women spend long years hiding, denying, burying, and pretending to be someone we are not. It chews deep wounds. It gnaws holes in the soul.

In the same vein, it may be impossible to share the utter joy that bathes our souls when we finally shed that masked costume and step into our own skin.

I carried that joy with me into the boundary waters. My canoe companions presumed that, like they, I was happy to be finishing school. But each paddle was a stroke of celebration of the newly discovered Ric. Each first glimpse of a lake horizon affirmed my pride in being alive and truly well. Each evening's bonfire burned vitality into my heart.

At the final night's campfire, I leapt up before my companions, grabbed a canoe paddle as a microphone, and sang "Ol' Man River." Having sung it in a high school song contest, I burst with deep and uproarious voice. That night I enjoyed a long, rousing applause, which pierced the serene darkness of the lakeshore woods.

The next morning, I peeled a small piece of white bark off a birch tree. On it, I penned a poem. I have since lost the poemed bark and remember only fragments. But from some new depth, the first and last lines of my coming-out poem:

At last, it's easy.
Finally—way down deep, it's easy.

Fifty years later, this still holds true. It is easy to be the person I am.

CHAPTER SEVENTEEN

HEART HOME

A Realization at the Dinner Table Last Night

"I am not the hub of my family anymore. Which is okay. I mean, we did it with my parents. It's natural. I'm getting used to it, but it's taking some adjusting." Connie is speaking about the family dinner shared last evening with her three sons, spouses, and grandchildren. A celebration of youngest son Gert's fortieth birthday.

As Honorary Uncle Ric, I am invited to family gatherings. Last night, two weeks after my second vaccine, I joined the family for a cook-out feast. Second son Torben and his partner, Cassandra, rent a charming old-style house, nestled in Niu Valley. With those intriguing indoor/outdoor spaces, I love gathering and eating with them. Having disappointed the family by turning COVID-driven thumbs-down on Thanksgiving gathering, it was my time to show up and enjoy.

I wore my mask as I entered the lānai—spurring Cassandra to scold me. "You take that mask off in my house!" She gave me her warm, full-body hug. "Where's Heno?"

"Connie uninvited him. She said the twins are afraid of dogs. He's at home pouting." I can play into drama.

"Ohhhh! I've told you before. Heno is always welcome in our home." Cassandra was winding up. I needed to change the topic, which I did.

One fraught unknown in this family gathering—how would the twins share space with the dogs? Kirsten and Kelly are afraid of dogs. Scream and jump into Daddy's arms kind of fear. Cassandra and Torben have two dogs. One might say two children with four legs. But the evening succeeded—no blowouts. Dogs went into a bedroom during dinner. Afterward, Cassandra sat with the girls and introduced them to doggies. Hands stretched out for a sniff and a pat on the head.

Trauma averted. Birthday celebrated. Grandma jubilant.

But it is true. I observed it myself. Connie is no longer the hub of the wheel. "Now it's four wheels, overlapping, but each one distinct on its own." I voiced my observation to her tonight and then added, "Family—be happy and thankful that you have time together."

No Winters, Living Near the Ocean, Mountain Views from my Windows

Those consequential reasons for moving to Hawai'i paled alongside that demanding inner voice, calling, "Ric, come! E komo mai. Hawai'i is your heart home!"

Yet, I am continually challenged that I may not really belong. Gathering for beers in the parking lot after *pau hana*—not my thing. Camping on the ground at Pōhakuloa to protest TMT, the proposed telescope, on Mauna Kea—I wouldn't be welcome. Revving the motor of a Toyota Tacoma jacked on a souped-up chassis with oversized wheels—that's not happening. Look at me—after thirty-four years in Hawai'i, I still look "Midwestern guy."

I tried so hard during my first decade in Hawai'i to belong. I took numerous Hawaiian language classes, but lacking a housemate who could 'ōlelo (speak), I never became fluent. With my Hawaiian partner and our Hawaiian clothing business, we befriended and socialized with people in hula hālau and Hawaiian entertainment. I got pretty good with my pidgin. My bookcase was filled with books on Hawaiian history and culture. Despite wanting to be Hawaiian, I wasn't, and there was nothing I could do about it.

All changed on a Sunday afternoon in 1998 when I sat with Aunty Vi outside the Naniloa Hotel beside Hilo Bay. Agreeing to teach me Hawaiian quilting, Aunty lit a fire in my soul that day. Reaching inside my mystery, she touched something deeper, something primal. My life clearly defined with that life-changing event, Aunty Vi took me and turned my heart inside out, adopting me into her family as her hānai son.

Following that day, my quest to belong shifted. I quit trying to become someone I could never be. Then and ever since, I am who I am. I am Ric Stark, the haole guy from Minnesota, who has adopted Hawai'i as his heart home. Like my art form of Hawaiian quilting, I am a blended person. I combine treasured traditions of both American and Hawaiian cultures—both in my quilting and in my being.

If I retain one "striving to become," then I strive to become a man who can embody and reflect the same beauty and gift that are born into my quilts. That, indeed, is enough.

I Swear

To tell the truth, always. (Well, almost always.) And the truth is it's not so much that I'm really that virtuous. I'm just such an open-book kind of guy that I simply can't get away with a lie.

You know the essay about sharing in the Larsen birthday celebration for Gert?

GOTCHA!

I wrote that on February 9 and shared it with Connie on Valentine's Day. Connie is one of three faithful friends reading my manuscript and giving me invaluable and (dammit) honest feedback to prompt my second, third, fourth…fourteenth editing.

At Denny's with our customary "ice teas with the blue stuff" (Equal sweetener), Connie began, "You know, I hate to pan a story about me, but I have to tell you, Ric. The story about Gert's birthday is missing something." (Okay, the one you just read is changed from the original version that I handed to Connie.)

She went on, "You know that I like your style of writing. I love your honesty. You're just a good man and your stories express that. But I don't know. Gert's birthday story—it's like you're telling it from the third person and you're not really in it."

"Dammit," I replied. "You're too insightful. I wanted to tell a story near the end that included you. Yes, I wrote that for you, not for me." Helpful feedback with the kind of brutal honesty that I invited and appreciate from my friend.

The trouble is—still—that I only spoke half the truth to Connie.

The story and that evening are about Connie's family. Don't get me wrong. The Larsens are wonderful people, great friends. I treasure my friendship with Connie—how it has deepened and ripened in the two years we have been neighbor buds.

But brutal honesty here—it's Connie's family that I gather and share time with. Not Ric's family.

In January 2017, my last and best relationship, with Johnny Pelanconi, ended. Six months later, Johnny passed from pancreatic cancer. Since 2017, I don't have a Ric's family. That hurts. I don't talk about it a lot. I may even write stories that pretend it doesn't matter.

I'm a guy with a big open heart and I love sharing that heart. And, again, don't get me wrong. I do share heart—with Nikki in California, with Connie next door, with friends in this senior complex, with coworkers from Bayada, with quilters in the Hawai'i Quilt Guild. Good friends, good sharing, good living.

But I don't have family of my own. I miss that. I refuse these days to go online to search for hook-up friends. Not interested.

I'm single and often alone. It's a vital, important, productive, rewarding time in my life. And it's a time without family around me.

I'm chastising myself here. Daniel Joshua Rubin speaks in my current read, *27 Essential Principles of Story*.[4] To paraphrase: Endings matter. At the end, answer the Central Dramatic Question, *Will Ric find belonging in Hawai'i?*, then finish and end it!

I mean, who wants to read a book without an ending? Another answer—a stronger one—plays in my head. Remember that earlier quote from Frances Kakugawa? "Once you begin to censor your work... you will lose the power of writing."[5]

The ending of this book would lose its power if I sell you the line that I've figured it all out and now I belong in Hawai'i, my true heart home. My story is unfinished. I'm still living it. I have bunches of stories lying on the editing floor, waiting to be shared. And I will share them.

It was easy for me to answer a call to Hawai'i. But *belonging*? That is a life-long voyage, and I'm still sailing mine. Same may be true of you. I am happy we shared this time together. Mahalo. Thank you.

So let us end with one simple, Hawaiian word. *Imua.* Forward.

---

4. Daniel Joshua Rubin, *27 Essential Principles of Story* (Workman Publishing, 2020).

5. Darien Gee, *Writing the Hawai'i Memoir* (Watermark Publishing, 2014).

HAWAIIAN GLOSSARY

Haole white person, American, Englishman, Caucasian
Hānai foster child, adopted child; foster, adopted
Heiau pre-Christian place of worship, shrine
Hālau long house, as for canoes or hula instruction;
          meeting house
Kahuna priest, sorcerer, expert in any profession
Kuiki quilting; to quilt
Kupuna grandparent, ancestor, relative or close
          friend of the grandparents' generation
Pali cliff
Liko leaf bud; newly opened leaf
Malihini stranger, foreigner, visitor
Mana spiritual power
'Ōlelo language; to speak
Pau finished, ended
Pau hana finished with work
Piko navel, navel string, umbilical cord
Pōhaku rock, stone
Pono goodness, uprightness, correct or proper
          procedure, excellence, well-being
Pueo Hawaiian owl

ACKNOWLEDGMENTS

How to express gratitude to the myriad folk who supported and contributed to a writing project fifty years in the making? "Ric, keep it simple."

My first mahalo must be extended to Darien Hsu Gee, my course instructor with Haliʻa Aloha, for giving me a pathway forward—out of doubt and confusion all the way to my own, real-live book for publishing. Thank you, Darien. Alongside, Dawn Sakamoto Paiva, director of sales and marketing with Legacy Isle Publishing, has contributed feedback and detailed answers to my too-many questions. Thank you, Dawn.

I owe reams of grateful shout-outs to three faithful friends who have accompanied me on this voyage. Their tireless, thoughtful editing has aided me to take a wordy manuscript, still lacking in "How does Ric feel about all this?" and to transform it into my goal—prose that sings like poetry. Thank you from the bottom of my heart, Connie Larsen, Nikki Bracken-Poe, and Penny Neuhaus.

Although he passed away two decades ago in Sac City, Iowa, I shout out a thank you to the heavens to Roy Ridge, my favorite teacher—the man who first recognized and encouraged a young lad to take up his skilled pen and to tell his story. Blessings, Mr. Ridge.

RIC D. STARK

Ric d. Stark is new to a post-retirement career in literary nonfiction. Inspired with a passion for creative writing in high school, Ric found his zest for the craft dimmed by a rigid college English composition professor. At age seventy-one, Ric resurrects the promise of a skilled pen with *Hawai'i Calling*. A graduate in 1976 with a Bachelor of Physical Therapy from the University of Minnesota in Minneapolis, Ric has worked in Hawai'i as a home health physical therapist for thirty-four years. Ric's first book, *Hawai'i Calling*, offers evidence that it is never too late to begin. Ric lives in Ewa Beach, Hawai'i, with his doggy, Heno.

ricdstark.com

Lightning Source UK Ltd.
Milton Keynes UK
UKHW020626240821
389389UK00012B/972

9 781948 011587